LIFE SKILLS

How To Make Your life Work Better, Be Wealthier, Healthier & Happier

Is your life running you?
Or are you running your life?

Brian H. Butler B.A., D.O.

Life Coach &
Pioneer of Kinesiology

http://ernestworkman.com

SUCCESS

MAKE YOUR LIFE WORK BETTER
AND BE WEALTHIER, HEALTHIER & HAPPIER!

Copyright © Brian H. Butler.
Revised edition published May, 2025.
ISBN: 978-1-7640294-2-1 Paperback.
ISBN: 978-1-7640294-3-8 E-Book.

All rights reserved. Without limiting the rights under copyright reserved above, no part of this publication may be reproduced, stored in or introduced into a database and retrieval system or transmitted in any form or by any means (electronic, mechanical, photocopying, recording or otherwise) without the prior written permission of the owner of the copyright.

Other books by the author:

https://www.amazon.com/stores/Brian-H.-Butler/author/B07J6S4PSK?ref=ap_rdr&isDramIntegrated=true&shoppingPortalEnabled=true

Your Breasts – What Every Woman Needs to Know NOW!
The Advanced Communications Training Workshop Manual
Balanced Health Textbook Volume I
Part II Advanced
An Introduction to Kinesiology
Kinesiology I
Advanced Kinesiology II
Who and What is God
Discover More About God
Why Are We Here

 Forty-five years ago, in the 1980's, I was fascinated with the content of many courses, tapes and seminars on "Personal Development and Success". I spent a lot of money and a great deal of time pursuing this interest.

Brian H. Butler   I bought many classics like "Think and Grow Rich" by Napoleon Hill, "How to win friends and influence people" and "The art of public speaking" by Dale Carnegie, "The 7 Habits of Highly Effective People" by Stephen R. Covey, "Nothing Down" by Robert Allen, "The Givers and the Takers" by Chris Evert and Bruce Feld, Atomic Habits" by James Clear - how to build good habits and break bad ones.

Many of these books had been written around 1935, the year I was born. The hundreds of principles all these books and tape programs contained were all 'keys' to greater success in every aspect of life.

Despite all this. I was not making the progress that I had hoped for. I was moderately successful, but I was not reaching the goals that all these resources suggested could be mine. I was puzzled.

I came to realise that the problem was my 'attitude'. I was learning all these skills, growing in knowledge, but I was not really putting the principles into practice daily in every situation in my life.

'Character Development' does not seem to be much in vogue in our era, but this book will provide you with many tools to improve your life.

Here are some important words which define 'character' that seem to have been allowed almost to disappear from common usage in our era.

Honesty, reliability, courtesy, punctuality, integrity, courage, patience, responsibility, kindness, compassion, confidence.

Many of the principles in the twelve chapters contained in this book you are holding may be new to you. When they are worked on diligently, and applied to every circumstance in your life, that practice will enable you to enjoy a more successful, wealthier, healthier, and happier life.

Brian H. Butler D.O., B.A., F.A.S.K.

≈ SUCCESS ≈

First Edition 1998

© Brian H. Butler 1998

©Life Skills Ltd., 1988

Brian H. Butler B.A.

All rights reserved. No parto of this publication may be reporoduced or transmitter in any form or by any means, electronic or mechanical, including photocopying, in in any information storage and retrieval system with out the express permission of th Author and the publishers.

The author does not accept any repsonsiblity, nor can he be held liable for any error of judgement of inacuracies in this book. It is dedigned to enbourage the reader and those intereseted in the subject to take more responsibility for their own lives.

In the case of any health matters or problems, nothing in this book should be taken as any suggestion to replace the consultation of a doctor, physician or a fully trained health professional.

The author has attempted to be fair, honest and sincere, and to comment from as objective a position as possible. The views expressed are the distillation bsed on the author's experience of many years of personal experience and earnest study.

Written, compiled and typeset by Brian H. Butler

Published by:

T.A.S.K.Books, 39, Browns Road, Surbiton, Surrey, KT5 8ST, U.K.

ISBN 0-9519279 -

Published with the assistance of Angel Key Publications
https://angelkey.com.au

Contents

Foreword	xiii
Preface	xv
Or why I wrote this program	xv
Personal Development Books And Tapes Inspired Me	xv
Why Wasn't I Becoming A Millionaire?	xv
It Was My Attitude And Perception That Held Me Back	xvi
Looking Back For A Minute	xvii
Then It All Changed	xix
Then It Happened!	xxi
Introduction	xxi
By Stephanie P. L. Mills. M.B.Ac.S.	xxiii
A Way To Program Your Mind For Success	xxiii
1. What This Book & Programme Will Do For You	**1**
So What Will This Book And Audio Seminar Program Do For You?	3
First: What Do You Think Holds Most People Back From Personal Success?	6
Second: This Is Called Self-Image & Self-Talk	7
Thirdly: Now Let's Consider Our Greatest Power! Choice	10
Are We Stuck Or Are We Free To Choose?	12
2. Personal Development - The Key To The Good Life	**15**
Firstly: The Key To Personal Development Is Change	15
Secondly: Take A Long-Term Overview Of Your Life	19
Thirdly. The Habit Of Daily Personal Growth & Development.	20

	The Three Simple Steps To Success –	22
	The 4th Step: Determining Your Sense Of Purpose.	27
	My Purpose Is:	28
	Some Ideas For Interaction With Others	25
	First Take Stock Of Your Life As You Are Today	26
3.	**Practical Steps Towards Achieving The Success You Desire**	**31**
	1. It Is Strong Desire That Fuels Your Drive For Success	32
	2. Fan The Flames Of Desire With Action	34
	2. Have A Written Plan - An Action List	36
	3. Work Your Plan	37
	4. "Keep A Log Or Journal Of All Your Work On Goals."	39
	5. Getting Started Each Day	40
	6. Work Smarter Not Harder	40
	7. The Power Of Review	41
4.	**Your Time Is Your Life - If I Only Had Time - Or How To Achieve More By Doing Less**	**47**
	Start To Move And Breathe More Slowly?	51
	Perhaps Begin To Speak More Slowly?	51
	Do Not Be Tempted To Over-Subscribe Your Time	52
	The Approval Trap - Giving Away Your Time	53
	On The Other Hand, Who Can You Give Some Time To?	53
	Punctuality: Being On Time Is One Way To Show Respect For Others	54
	Meeting People And Clients - Punctually!	56
	Allow Extra Time For Things To Go Wrong	56
	Block Interruptions	56
	Each Day, First Prepare Yourself For The World	57
	Choose What You Like To Do Best	57

	Know What Time You Do What Best	58
	Where Do You Do What Work Best?	58
	Categorise And Prioritize Tasks	58
	Time Is Your Most Valuable Asset	58
	Procrastination Is The Thief Of Time.	59
	We Need To Arrange To Have Time For Others	59
	Live In The Present	59
	Take Time To Appreciate And Enjoy The "Now Moments"	60
	We All Need "Down Time" - And Time For Ourselves	61
5.	**Your Health, Happiness, And Prosperity**	**63**
	Safeguard Your Health	63
	You Can't Work Well If You Don't Feel Well!	65
	1. Eating For Health	67
	2. Nutritional Supplements	69
	3. It Pays To Watch What You Drink	69
	4. Stress Is A Killer	70
	5. Exercising And Breathing	71
	6. Rest And Relaxation	76
	7. Sleep	76
	Take Action Now If You Do Not Feel 100% Well	77
	Prevention Is Better Than Cure!!	78
6.	**Listening With Power And Attention**	**79**
	Avoid Being In Control, And Be A Leader.	79
	Agree Wherever Possible Or Agree To Disagree	80
	Avoid Judgmental Or Critical Statements.	82
	The First Interaction	82
	Initial Stages Of Communication	83
	The Power Of Silence	84

	Listen 70% - Talk 25% - Pause 5%	85
	Use Open Questions That Start With How, Who, What, Where, & When	85
	Avoid Closed Questions	86
	What To Do If The Conversation Dies	86
	Interrupting - Don't	86
	No-No Responses	87
	Yes-Yes Responses	87
	Watch Out For Semantics	87
	Manners Maketh Man	89
	Listening And Caring Builds Trust	89
	Keeping In Touch - Showing That You Have "Heard" Their Need	91
7.	**The Scourge Of The 4-Letter Word**	**95**
	Proceed With Caution	95
	Improving Our Inter-Personal Communication	97
	Recognizing The Desire To Control	99
	Twelve Common Types Of Communication That Do Not Work Well.	100
	Relinquishing The Desire To Control	102
	The Four Letter Words	103
	Caution - Use This Information Carefully	106
8.	**People Talk In "Code"**	**109**
	Going "Under The Code" And Listening To Decode The "Code"	110
	Remember - Listen For Announcements	111
	People Reveal Themselves And Their Feelings By What They Say	112
	Go Under The Code, But Do Not Pry	112
	The Power Of Feel-Want-Willing	113

CONTENTS

	Introducing A Neutral Third Party	115
	Active Listening - A Powerful Communications Tool	115
	Useful Active Listening Responses.	118
	When Should Active Listening Be Used	119
	Why Should The Person Solve His Own Problem	119
	Under What Conditions Should Active Listening Be Used	119
	What Are The Common Errors In Using Active Listening	120
	What Attitude Should You Have When You Active Listen	120
	What Happens To The Other Person When You Active Listen Correctly	121
	Knowledge - Understanding - Wisdom	121
	Knowledge	122
	Understanding	122
	Wisdom	123
	Conclusion	124
9.	**Money, Prosperity And Wealth**	**125**
	Money Makes The World Go Round	125
	Make Financial Independence One Of Your Goals	125
	The Allure Of "Easy Money".	127
	Becoming A Millionaire, Or At Least Well-Off - By Saving!	128
	Avoid "Instant Gratification"	130
	Spend Now - Pay Later, The Seductive Fliers Cry	130
	Watch Those Credit Cards!	131
	Here Is The Opposite Of Spend Now - Pay Later	132
	Be Your Own Loan Shark!	133
	Buying Your Home	133
	Beware Of Being A Guarantor	136

If You Are Employed, Make Yourself Indispensable.	136
Start Thinking Now About Having Your Own Business One Day	137

10. More Money, Prosperity And Wealth — 141

Seed Sowing To Grow Your New Business	141
Success In Life Is A Numbers Game	141
Business Cards Are A Valuable Tool - Winners Use Them Freely!	142
Expand Your Contacts, Sell Yourself To As Many People As Possible	142
Storing Names And Addresses And Printing Letters & Mail Labels	143
Sell Yourself - How? Be Concerned About Your Customers!	145
When Your Business Builds, As Soon As You Can - Get Help!	145
Speculate To Accumulate	147
Everything Has To Make A Profit	148
Don't Give Your Stuff Away	148
Sell The Sizzle, Or The Taste, Or The Smell, Or The Feel....	148
Post Sales Reassurance	149
Be Aware, Everyone Knows A Lot Of People - So Keep Clients Happy!	150
Accounting And Records	151
Pay Your Bills - And Smile!!!	151
What About Paying Tax?	153

11. Happiness Is An Attitude Of Mind + Positive Action   157

Happiness Is An Attitude Of Mind + Positive Action	157
Short Term Induced "Happiness"	158
Making Others Happier Helps Us Feel Happier	159
Ensuring We Have A Steady Supply Of "Happy"	161
You Cannot Regret Achieving Something Worthwhile	161
Self-Discipline Increases Productivity	162
Aesthetic Appreciation	163
Encouraging And Feeding The Higher Self	164
Getting The Mind To Flourish And Produce Fruits Of Success	165
Start With A Mental Spring Clean	166
Picture What You Really Want!	167
Visualization Works! If You Visualize Negative Things, Then That Is What You Produce. If You Focus On Picturing Positive Changes In Your Life, Then That Is What You Will Bring To Yourself.	167
Happiness Increases Productivity And Wealth	168
Finding Happiness In Love And True Values	169
Foundations To Build Happy, Loving Relationships On Respect	169
Acceptance	170
Communication	170
It Takes Two	170
Joyful Love - The Opposite Of The Misery Of Infatuation	170
Love Is... The Way To True Happiness	171

12. Here's To Your Wealth, Health And Happiness   173

To Be Wealthy - Think Big, But Start Small	173
To Be Wealthy - Develop Thoughts And Thinking Power	173
Think Wealthy - Open A "Prosperity Account"	174

To Be Wealthy - Watch Your Untouchable Savings Grow	174
Become Prosperous - Open A "Capital Account"	174
Build Your Capital For Wealth, Health And Happiness	175
Be Wealthier - Expect To Win. Ten Ways To Prepare	176
Be Successful	177
Be Healthier Twelve Ways To Build Your Health	177
Be Healthier - How To Stay Young And Live Longer	178
How Old Are We?	179
Be Healthier - Eight Routines That Affect Longevity	180
Be Happier - How To Stay Young And Live Longer	180
Maturity Of Mind	181
Be Healthier - Ten Words To Meditate On	182
Be Happier - Use These Dynamics With Others	182
Be Happier - On The Subject Of Relationships	182
Givers And Takers	183
On The Subject Of Happiness	183
Be Happier - Express Gratitude	184
Be Happier - Expect Good Things To Happen And They Will.	185
Call To Action	185
In Your Wildest Dreams - Think The Impossible Dream	186

Arrive Early, Breath, Visualize, Smile And Enjoy   **189**

Appendix   **191**
  Resource Addresses   191
    Kinesiology In Great Britain   191
    Kinesiology In Ireland   191

FOREWORD

By: Dr. Sheldon C. Deal N.D., D.C.

I have been an avid reader and listener of success and motivational material for 40 years. Consequently, I have acquired a large number of books and tapes on the subject. I listen to 300 tapes per yot 300 different tapes, because the good ones I will listen to over and over. It is said if you listen to a tape seven times, you own the material on that tape.

So why am I telling you all this? Because in all my years of pursuing this subject, never have I come across such a complete and concise coverage of this material as Brian Butler has put together. He has added new insights and refreshing ideas to these age old-age principles.

His sincerity and honesty come through quite clearly as you cover the material. Usually when I get a new album of tapes I have become quite adept at picking out the one or two new ideas or principles being advocated by the author. However in this case, Mr. Butler has crammed in so many of the steadfast ideas that one would have had to spend years collecting all this material otherwise.

Unlike many authors on these topics who have achieved multi- millionaire status which can be intimidating to the new student, Mr. Butler comes from a perspective of being in the trenches and making it work.

I have known Mr. Butler for 20 years, and I am here to tell you that he is a successful student of his own philosophy. His style is such as to include a checklist at the end of each section which can be very helpful to the student. A helpful hint for you is when you finish each section, share what you have learned with someone and the fact that you are making an expression will help you to make a lasting impression on your own being. This will go a long way to help you make the material become part of your own make up.

This book, "How to Make Your Life Work Better" represents the best of the best. Try it, you'll like it.

Dr. Sheldon C. Deal.
Author and lecturer.

PREFACE

Or why I wrote this program

PERSONAL DEVELOPMENT BOOKS AND TAPES INSPIRED ME

Many books and audio systems abound on the subject of personal development. Most of them are written by very successful people, many telling the story of ordinary folk who have risen to positions of power in commerce and industry. They are produced in the main by very wealthy people, who want to pass on to others the secrets of their success.

As a young man, I read all the classics in the field self improvement I could find:

- "How to Win Friends and Influence People" by Dale Carnegie,
- "Think and Grow Rich", by Napoleon Hill,
- "How to Think Like a Millionaire"
- "The Art of Public Speaking"
- "Nothing Down" by Robert Allen to name but a few.

My taped voice hero was Earl Nightingale. Just to listen to his rich dark brown voice, as he talked about success and how to achieve it, sent shivers up my spine. I used to listen to all his tapes, and other audio programmes from Nightingale Conant, on every aspect of business, life, wealth, health, and happiness. Earl Nightingale was an amazing inspiration to me, and so were many of the other speakers I listened to during those early years.

WHY WASN'T I BECOMING A MILLIONAIRE?

The problem was, I did not turn those priceless words about all the concepts that ensure success into action as soon as I heard or read them. The result was that my life went on pretty much the same as most average people's life does.

Although I got a lot out of those programmes, something was missing for me. Somehow, I could not bridge the mind gap between those authors who were right at the top of the tree, and where I found myself, pretty near the very bottom. I found myself thinking, what lucky breaks did they have that they don't mention? I wonder, was their father rich and helped them on the way? How did they get from worker to CEO?

IT WAS MY ATTITUDE AND PERCEPTION THAT HELD ME BACK

I have to say very clearly, that this was my MISPERCEPTION. I got it very wrong. Whatever their lives had in the way of "luck" or the "silver spoon", had absolutely nothing to do with the fact that I was not as successful as they were.

> **The problem was ME.**
> **It was MY attitude that**
> **was bent out of shape.**

I was working very hard, and by standards then, I was making a great deal of money, but I just could not get into their mind set. I could not make the mental leap from being quite well off as a salesman to being a millionaire driving a Rolls Royce. It did not dawn on me how I could possibly get from a) to b).

What was wrong?

My conditioning was very strong that I did not belong "up there". I constantly limited myself by my own feelings. I felt frustrated that there seemed to be a very real ceiling, above which I just could not break through. Let's face it; I got in my own way.

In my late forties, I found myself pretty much struggling to survive with two mortgages, and all the usual bills. So I started to review all the old audios and books I had studied previously….. but now I began to apply what I read. In consequence my financial position has changed dramatically.

PREFACE

I suddenly realized that I might have something that struggling young people might benefit from. My over forty five years in business, and just living this life, have taught me a lot. I have made more than my fair share of tactical errors in my life, which could have been avoided quite simply.

If I had someone like me to relate to when I was younger, someone who was not so far above me that it seemed impossible to attain the success they had, I might have done better. **We can all benefit from a mentor!**

So I decided to create this program, as someone who is now successful. I want to share with others how I made the transition from struggling along never having quite enough for the exotic holidays, cars, or houses; to making a lot more money, and being in a much stronger financial position.

I am sure you will find hundreds of useful tips in these pages, and when you listen to my voice. Buy MP3's online. I know you will be inspired and realize that it really is possible for you make dramatic changes in your life. All you have to do, is to **ACTION** what you read and hear. Think **BIG** and start small! Use the tools in this book and audio files, and you will prosper as I have.

LOOKING BACK FOR A MINUTE

Expelled from school at sixteen, for a very minor misdemeanor, I fulfilled a dream I had since I was eight years old, and went onto a farm as a pupil. There I was introduced to life in the raw pretty quickly. The farmer was committing adultery with a neighbor, whilst beating up his wife! And his sister of fifty four made passionate advances to me. I learned a little about farming, and a lot about life. Not long later I was then conscripted into Her Majesty's Forces, where I was given some intensive training in the electronics of ground radar. I found the concepts of the vast power of electricity, and how it could be manipulated in circuitry to do practically anything to be totally fascinating.

After I had served my national service I went to work in a building society where my then fiancée worked. My father had continually insisted that I should get a "safe, secure, pensionable job". That view he impressed upon me probably emanated from his own concerns for security.

My father had entered the First World War at eighteen, as a very proud volunteer. He, like millions of other British lads, felt very strongly about the right of our nation to rule itself, and that the bullies in Germany had to be stopped from ruining the lives of so many millions in Europe. It was only a few months before he was "at the front", and only a matter of days before he went "over the top", only to be mown down like millions of others.

My father was "lucky", he only lost his right leg, not his life. This brave man later married, and his wife bore two children. Sadly she died in childbirth having the second. He then married my mother. Naturally, with three children to support, he was very concerned about job security.

So I found work as a representative in a building society, visiting estate agents and bank managers who then sent us people who wanted mortgages and investment advice. It was a 'safe job; and carried a pension. This was interesting enough at first.

However it was not long before I was "head hunted" by one of the agents I visited, but after a couple of years of showing people around houses I sought something more challenging.

I then joined a company as a salesman that sold perforated structural steel that was used to fabricate shelving, racking, benches, and mezzanine floors. I reveled in the design aspects of space saving, and enjoyed drawing schemes on my pad in front of factory managers, and office executives. I finally was enjoying my work, and becoming very successful!

It was not long before my monthly sales total exceeded that of the other thirteen salesmen. In my own time, and at my own expense, I had attended some sales training courses, and of course, read a lot about selling in books. I did put some of the things I learned into practice, but sadly not all of them. Pretty soon, the management wanted to promote me. I then was given the title of Area Supervisor, with several salesmen under my care.

PREFACE

The financial terms were interesting. As is so often the case, the company thought they would economize on the rather large commission checks I was receiving. And so although my basic salary went up, my commission structure went down. The net result was, that as an "executive", I was earning less than I did as a salesman!

This was rather short sighted of the company, but it was pretty much standard practice in those days. I went to the managing director, explained the situation, and asked him if I should stay or go. They gave me back my old territory I had as a salesman, with exactly the same commission arrangements, I also retained my "executive" position with its higher salary, plus I still had an override on my salesmen's efforts. Now I really started to earn **serious** money again.

Unhappily though, I also learned about the average salesman's attitude to life. I would make an appointment to meet them at 8.30 a.m. on their territory, to instruct them in salesmanship. The salesman might turn up at 9.00, or 9.15 mumbling something about the trains or the traffic. The number of calls they usually made was pathetic. None of them reached the monthly target very often. The firm started a prize incentive scheme. We would get one point per pound up to our target, and fifty points when we went over the target. The monthly target in those days was a thousand pounds in orders. The first month of the prize scheme I sold £5400! Nobody else reached the £1000 target. I won a lot of prizes.

THEN IT ALL CHANGED
Something was ticking away in my head during the last few years. I was about twenty five years old at the time. My wife was expecting her first baby and although I was making a lot of money by employee standards, something was missing. I felt empty.

It appeared to me that the world was going badly wrong.

Even after the "War to end all wars" was over, there were still about forty five wars going on! The famine, the disease, poverty, man's inhumanity to man... It all looked pretty black out there. But what I did not realise was that although all the above was true, my ability to keep it in proportion and balance was leaving me.

I was the archetypical "Whizz kid", I was working eight days a week, twenty six hours a day, and consuming two cups of strong coffee to the hour. I did the selling in the day, and erected steel structures in the evenings and weekends so I was making a lot of money, but burning myself out in the process. And even now in the 21st Century it seems, the more able and intelligent a young person is, the more likely they are to follow this pattern.

So I resigned my job, bought a twenty acre farm, moved in, and within a couple of weeks, had a nervous breakdown. (As one does!) My wife with our new baby, did not appreciate the move, and said so. We sold the farm, and moved back into suburbia. I went back to my old job as a lowly salesman again. However this time I found it harder. Something was still ticking away in my head. I still felt like a hollow shell. I then came across a charity which seemed to be doing a lot about the state of the world. They seemed to have some practical answers to a lot of the world's problems. So I applied for a job and was taken on. I also was able to take a four year full time bachelor of arts degree course while I was with them. This again meant working days, evenings and weekends. It was not easy, but it was very worthwhile.

I stayed with that organization until I was forty, when without any warning, I was "let go, "downsized", "made redundant or "sacked". Whatever you call it, it means, NO JOB. They closed my department, and that was that. I was devastated, I went home and cried. I thought "this is the end of my life!

Working for a charity for all those years, my earnings had been pitifully small. I had virtually no savings whatever. I had made a conscious choice to put money last in my life, while I concentrated on matters of developing the character and the spirit.

What on earth shall I do now? One thing I decided most emphatically,

≈ PREFACE ≈

I would never again put myself in a position where someone could terminate my livelihood.

That meant I had to be self employed. I went to America and studied the new health art/science of Applied Kinesiology.

I then became an instructor of a revolutionary health programme for lay people. I returned to the UK, and began to spread the word about this most remarkable new concept to anyone who would listen.

Progress was excruciatingly slow. But after a few years I finished up teaching groups all over Britain, and in many countries in Europe, Happily, I was now much in demand as a practitioner and as a result the clinic side of my business began to develop. I was training more practitioners, and running classes to teach people about basic kinesiology.

But regrettably, my wife and I had grown apart, and my marriage broke up. I finished up with virtually nothing of the assets I had worked all my life for. It meant that I had to start all over again in mid life! As many people do.

THEN IT HAPPENED!

I was nearly fifty, virtually having to start over from square one. So I got out all the books and tapes, and this time, I began to apply more of what I read.

In hindsight my progress over the next decade and a half was quite remarkable. In that time I built several successful businesses. Everything has been working very well for me as success came towards me in a fast and accelerating mode.

However, I am now not so far removed from my old struggle, or my self-destructive attitudes that I cannot remember very clearly where I went wrong. I just could not get my head around it back then, but now it is a very different ball game.

So over time it became very important for me to share my change of attitude, the knowledge, understanding, and the wisdom I have developed in my latter years. I really wanted to help others who are younger than I am. I want to save you a lot of wasted time and grief.

Study this programme, and action it. As soon as you have mastered its contents, keep reviewing it, and keep learning, growing and putting what you learn into ACTION.

That way, you WILL join me in becoming wealthier, healthier, and happier.

Brian H. Butler

INTRODUCTION

By Stephanie P. L. Mills. M.B.Ac.S.

A WAY TO PROGRAM YOUR MIND FOR SUCCESS

Are circumstances and events in your life controlling you? Or are you controlling the circumstances and events in your life? Would you like to be more successful? Wealthier? Healthier? Happier?

Mr. Butler has gathered a wealth of knowledge and experience during his nearly forty years in business. He has studied endless volumes on personal development, attended numerous seminars, and listened to inspirational tapes from many of the "greats" in diverse fields of endeavor. He has taught public speaking, business and personal communication skills, and the art of selling for nearly thirty years.

This program is a distillation of all that study and involvement. That means that the material in this program is highly concentrated. Hundreds of books have been written on all these topics covered here, and the collected pearls of wisdom you are about to be exposed to, are a treasure beyond price. However, only as information is put to use is it of any real value.

It is his earnest desire to share the application of the wisdom he has gleaned. Although by dint of a lot of hard work, by making many mistakes, and sometimes failing to implement what he knew to be a better course of action, he has made a success of several businesses.

The purpose of this program is to prepare your mind for success. Although you may currently be doing reasonably well, the concepts offered will perhaps show you a very different way to think from the way you do now. It will enable you to achieve even more in your life both in the sphere of success, wealth and health, but also in the all important area of human values and the natural laws which govern the development of the human spirit.

The concepts, the many aphorisms and adages contained in this program are all of priceless value. As you absorb and utilize the ideas and suggestions offered, you will begin to be in a much better position to make more of your life.

Each tiny step you take in a positive way, will bring its own rewards. Then as and when you are ready, you will be able to go out into the market place, and sort the wheat from the chaff and find your own way to wealth health and happiness.

In no way is this intended to promote a "get rich quick" scheme. It is not a "business opportunity" at all in the usual sense of the word, although there is a way to increase your own personal "education account". Also, as you implement the principles herein, you will definitely prepare yourself to take advantage of any genuine business plan you may come across. You will also work steadily towards financial independence.

This program is designed to help you become the type of person that will be a success in what ever you set your hand to do. Regardless of the job you are in, or the business you start and develop, you will succeed better by practicing these concepts. The universal principles offered in this book and audio files will work no matter what calling or type of work you choose.

Hundreds of business opportunities abound. They all seem to promise hundreds a week for only a few hours work. Perhaps some of them fulfill their promises.

But what is the main problem that stops you going into business for yourself? What is the main obstacle that prevents you from expanding and developing a business you already have?

It is because of the way we think. It is also due to the way we do not think. You are not what you think, but what you think - you are! As a man thinks in his inner being, so he is. Thoughts always precede accomplishment. The chair you are sitting on started its life as a thought in the mind of the designer.

INTRODUCTION

We are not the way we are by accident, or bad luck, or any other external force. Your life and mine are the direct result of what we think, and how we act on what we think.

To change the way our life is, we have to think differently. To grow rich we have to think in an entirely different way. The main obstacle to success and happiness lies in our own lack of ability to learn the laws of success, and put them into practice.

If you always do what you have always done, you will always get what you've always got!

To achieve a change in your reality, it is necessary to change your perception of how life works. Or put another way, as you change your perception of the factors that make your life the way it is, you will change the reality of the way you are.

Having worked with Mr. Butler for over twenty years, I have reaped the benefit of applying his wisdom in my own life. My business has prospered, and my savings have grown. I wish you all the best for you in your own life as you make them work for you.

Stephanie P. L. Mills

CHAPTER ONE

WHAT THIS BOOK & PROGRAMME WILL DO FOR YOU

Hello, my name is Brian Butler
This program is about:
How To Make Your Life Work Better And Be Wealthier, Healthier, And Happier!

Not many years ago, I had to scrimp and save to get by. Bills usually caused me a certain amount of anxiety. Like most people, there always seemed to be too much month for the money.

As a young man I started to listen to audio tapes, study material written by successful people, and attend training courses in personal development. The principles they outlined were always fascinating, even exciting, but somehow I did not always manage to apply their ideas in my life.

In a way, multi-millionaires telling me I could be rich if I would just do this and that, only seemed to serve to frustrate me further. "It's all right for them", I used to think. It is easy when you have a lot of money to make more. Many of them told how they started from very humble and poor beginnings, but I just could not always relate to their stories.

Often they seemed to leave out the main pieces of the story, or it appeared their success was all due to lucky breaks. This was not always true, but it was my perception. It was that incorrect perception that held me back for years.

I had missed the point. I did not apply each principle I learned as soon as I came across it.

I read ever more books on personal development, and listened to yet more tapes on success. I still wasn't a millionaire, very far from it! But, I realized I was beginning to make progress both financially, and also in my understanding of life skills and values.

Then something began to dawn on me. Almost without realizing it, I was beginning to put more of the vital key principles into practice. The constant repetition was getting the laws of success into my mind. I began to appreciate that I was not struggling financially to make ends meet like I used to.

I had been steadily building a successful business during a time when five thousand small traders were going bust every year. I had two homes in England and one in the United States, a top of the range car with all the luxurious extras here, and a Cadillac in the U.S.A. Now I live in a very prosperous area of Western Australia with my lovely wife. Although I am retired, I have continued dramatically to increase my personal wealth, my health continues to be robust, and I am truly happy.

I am now in my eighth decade, as was Colonel Sanders when he finally made a huge success of Kentucky Fried Chicken. I am not yet a worldwide franchiser like he became, but I did become a successful businessman. I want to share with others why I have succeeded now, when for years I was "stuck". I want to save you some long-term grief. As my business and my success has grown, I have had an increasing desire to help others achieve the same. Several people have been kind enough to thank me for giving them keys which have resulted in their enjoying greater success in their lives.

So I decided to create a program to help anyone who wants to change their lives for the better. It takes work and guts to make changes in your life. Nothing about changing your life is easy, but it certainly IS worthwhile. You can start using the building blocks to success immediately, as you implement what you learn in this book and audio files.

My aim is to help those in their twenties, thirties and forties, or indeed any age, to find greater success and happiness in their lives. I want to share my experiences over forty-five years. I want to spare others the grief of having to reinvent the wheel over and over again. I know now where I went wrong in many ways.

I now realize that had I implemented certain key principles sooner, and fallen in line with fundamental laws of success earlier, I would have been a millionaire many times over long before now.

So here is the distillation of all the tapes and books I have devoured with interest, but not acted on soon enough.

You would have to read many dozens of books and listen to hundreds of hours of tapes to cover the material covered in this one program. So take advantage of the work I have done to summarize it all for you. Then go read, listen to, and attend more programs yourself, so that you continue learning.

As soon as I did start to apply these laws of success in my own life, I became happier, healthier and more prosperous much quicker than I ever thought I would.

Read this book, listen to the audio files, follow what it says carefully, and above all apply it.

Change the way you think now, and it will work for you.

SO WHAT WILL THIS BOOK AND AUDIO SEMINAR PROGRAM DO FOR YOU?

What you are doing with your life may be OK, and I want to offer you suggestions you might use to extend yourself. Suggestions designed to enhance your development, your wealth, health, and happiness. There may be many things you might be able to do better. Doing less than your very best slowly erodes the character. Our outer world is always a reflection of the inner world of our minds.

The fundamental truths laid out in these chapters will change your life - but only if you put them to work for you. They will bring you more money, greater success, better health, personal recognition, and improve your relationships with friends and family.

A screwdriver will not drive screws in, nor will a saw cut wood by themselves. Unless these tools are taken out of the toolbox and used wisely and energetically in skilled hands, they are of no real value. Sick fish drift downstream. Lively fish swim upstream, and even leap up waterfalls to reach their ultimate goal. It is all too easy for us to take the lazy way out, and let life drift by. There is plenty to while away your time. TV, magazines, newspapers, the pub...

Has your life changed significantly in the last five years? Where will you be five or ten years from now? Will you be living in much the same way in the years ahead, as you are now? If you want to be a success, you can be. Take stock of your life now. Where are you at? Are you where you want to be in life? If not, why do you think that is? If you do not like where you are - change it. If you do not like where you live - change it. If you do not like your job - change it.

What are you going to do today to make a significant difference in your life starting today?

Within each one of us there is a spark of genius! All you need to cause this spark to start your success engine is to provide the fuel of DESIRE.

Allow this information to stimulate you, encourage you, enlighten you, and fill you with enthusiasm for your own personal development.

You can change. Your life can improve dramatically. All you have to do is apply the immutable laws of the universe to your daily life. Then, suddenly, things will begin to improve. Step by step, you will leave behind the ineffective habits of the life you now have, and you will forge a brand new, stronger you. Your everyday ways of thinking will change. This will result in a different approach.

**The change in your approach will cause you to have different thoughts. You will develop the
DESIRE which will fuel these thoughts into ACTION.**

Your new actions will bring you different, more productive and beneficial results. It is impossible for them not to. We daily create our own circumstances. Many people wonder why they are poor and unhappy. They feel they have had a raw deal in life, and there is not much they can do about it. That may be true of a few unfortunates, but most people could change their lives for the better dramatically, if they only knew how. Most do not appreciate that the unseen immutable laws cannot be broken with impunity. Those who disregard many of the basic spiritual laws of life, wonder why they reap the result of unhappy, unsuccessful, poverty stricken lives. Individuals, who ignore these fundamental truths, do so at their own peril.

You can decide at any time to change your life. It is never too late, but the earlier you start the better. You can join the tiny proportion of people who ACT on what they learn.

The fact that you purchased this program puts you in the top 5% of the population. Implement the ideas in this and other programs with enthusiasm, and that will put you in the top 1%! The instant you begin to get into harmony with natural laws, your life will change for the better. Maybe slowly at first, but nevertheless, things will start to "go your way".

It is only to the extent that you apply the principles outlined that you will start to benefit. One thing is certain, repetition is the mother of memory, and of new habits. Listen to this program regularly. Read the manual often, and sometimes read along while listening to the audio files at the same time. Listen in the car when you are stuck in traffic. This way, the golden rules will become part of your thinking and your mindset more rapidly and more effectively. We are going to cover three topics in this section:

"Self-Esteem", "Self-Talk", and our greatest power - **CHOICE**.

FIRST: WHAT DO YOU THINK HOLDS MOST PEOPLE BACK FROM PERSONAL SUCCESS?

Lack of self-esteem is the world's most prevalent sickness, and it holds most people back from achieving greater success in their lives. Less than 3% of the world's well educated population sets any goals. Those that do have a high self-esteem and good sense of self-worth.

The rest of the population has varying degrees of low self-esteem. When does this situation begin? At birth, or even before! Scientific studies show that unborn babies in the womb are affected greatly by their mother's attitude towards the pregnancy. Children that are unwanted, or who are conceived under difficult circumstances such as rape, appear to do less well than those who are very much wanted. A baby towards the full term is aware of all the noises and moods of the people around it. If the parents do not get on, or the mother herself is unhappy, and suffers from low self- esteem, this appears partially to be transmitted to the unborn baby.

The birth process comes as a great shock to the child. One moment they are in a warm bath, then someone pulls out the plug, and there they are wondering what is going on!

The next minutes or hours in the babies' life are probably as uncomfortable as they are for the mother who is giving birth. The pressure and pain involved in squeezing the infant down the birth canal must be very considerable for both parties.

Then once into the new world of bright lights and loud noises, with the first breath, the baby usually lets everyone know of its pain and disapproval of the whole process. Whether or not birth has a profoundly negative effect on the newborn child's self-esteem depends upon many factors.

In the complementary medicine modality of applied kinesiology there are many ways to address emotional problems and especially the birth trauma. In dealing with many thousands of people over twenty-five years, practitioners recognize a very high proportion of clients need to release the negative aspects of their birth experience. Releasing birth trauma, which usually is quite simply achieved in one or two sessions, often results in an amazing change in the person's confidence and self-esteem.

Regrettably, parents often inadvertently reduce their offspring's self-esteem by undue or excessive criticism. Many schoolteachers are responsible for the systematic destruction of self-esteem. When "Could do better." Appears too many times on reports, it does nothing to help the child improve. Peer pressure, comparing self with others, failure to achieve, all progressively reduce a child's sense of self-worth. Some have estimated that the average child leaves school with about 15% of the self-esteem and self-worth they were born with. Of course there are exceptions.

Anyhow, based on the above, the chances are you do not have as high a measure of self-worth as you might. On the positive side though, you are to be commended in that you have bought this program, and to be congratulated for looking for ways to develop yourself.

SECOND: THIS IS CALLED SELF-IMAGE & SELF-TALK
Now let's look at how the internal chatter, or 'self-talk' that goes on in our brains ceaselessly, can work against us. One way we keep our self-esteem in tatters is the negative way we talk to ourselves internally. We talk ourselves down, much more than most people realize. Constantly mumbling apologies, or criticizing ourselves is disastrous.

> **Once we recognize that it is highly destructive to talk to ourselves negatively, it will help us to begin the process of repairing the damage.**

Positive "SELF-TALK" involves practicing saying things to yourself which build you up rather than tear you down. Most people talk to themselves very negatively, and even rudely and insultingly. "I am an idiot", "I am useless" etc. It is essential to begin to reverse this destructive habit, NOW. That is if we are to become a real success. From earliest childhood, we learn from others that it is wrong to speak well of yourself. That may well be true. An ancient proverb says, "Let another praise you, not your own mouth."

BUT, just because it is not a good idea to praise yourself, it is certainly not good to criticize yourself, run yourself down, or tell yourself and others that you are no good at this or that.

Typical self-talk statements are:

- I'm hopeless at math.
- I can't draw for toffee.
- I'm useless at ball games.
- I can't hold a tune.
- I never was able to draw.
- I couldn't learn another language.
- I just can't remember names.
- I never get that right. I'm always making mistakes.
- That's just like me, clumsy! I'm always dropping things.

Even if any of the above things are true of you historically, there is no need to reinforce the idea in your mind. Your subconscious is always listening to you, and to what you say, and making an almost indelible record of it.

The more often you say something, the deeper that concept is burned into the subconscious mind. These records with a very negative bias affect everything you do, or attempt to do. They hold you in a pattern of being "useless" or whatever, **FOR THE REST OF YOUR LIFE,** unless dealt with!

The opposite is also true. The more often we repeat positive statements either silently or out aloud, the more deeply they are etched into our psyche. If we are to become the best we can be, and of value to this world, it is essential to have good self-esteem. If we value ourselves highly, we are in a better position to grow ourselves, and more able to bring worthwhile values to others.

We have been conditioned since youth to regard self-love and self-praise as big-headed, vain or just "not done". I was shocked when I realized that: **We can only love others to the extent that we love and appreciate the good in ourselves.** When we view in ourselves the character traits we do not want, we sometimes allow this to depress us and make ourselves miserable. This leads to self-talk which further creates a downward spiral.

Forgive yourself for being less than you would like to be and plod on with joy in your heart. You now know that unlike most people, you are not only recognizing where change is desirable, you are actually doing something about it.

These negative mental records used to be very difficult to change. Thankfully now, Kinesiologists have many tools to help us re-write the mis-statements we have learned to accept about ourselves, and make immediate and permanent changes.

Now you are aware of the principle of self-talk, you can turn it to your advantage and say only positive things about yourself. You do not have to praise yourself, but you can say, "I am really working at remembering people's names", or "Although I have never thought I could draw, I am taking classes and really enjoying the experience." "I am not nearly as clumsy as I used to be."

Affirmations can reduce the deepest seated of all problems, and address our basic lack of love and confidence for and in ourselves. It helps to affirm regularly out aloud: "I profoundly and deeply accept and love myself with all my problems and shortcomings".

It also works well to vary what you actually say. You might want to say something like: "I love myself with all my faults and failings", or "I deserve to be happy, and feel good about myself". Of course you can make up your own phrases or sentences that suit your particular circumstances.

If you do this on a regular basis, it will help to reinforce a more positive type of "Self-Talk", and you will slowly but surely re-program your mind. Encourage yourself on a daily basis to listen for and eradicate all negative self-talk. You can systematically rebuild your self-esteem as you take control of your life, and enjoy many mini-successes along the way.

THIRDLY: NOW LET'S CONSIDER OUR GREATEST POWER! CHOICE

Efforts to work on ourselves will be stifled unless we **believe and accept** that we have the ability, (and the responsibility) to make choices concerning every aspect of our lives, especially when we think we have no choice.

HUMAN BEINGS GREATEST POWER IS CHOICE

Each day, we all make thousands of choices like:

- Shall I do this . . . or that?
- Eat this . . . or not?
- Buy this model of car . . . or a different one?
- Live here . . . or move?
- Smoke . . . or give it up!
- Cross the road now . . . or later!
- Or more important ones like:
- Stay in this job . . . or leave
- Get another job, or start a business.
- Stay married . . . or get divorced.

Yet, a thought persists in most people's minds: I HAVE to do this, or I've GOTTA do that. So in a sense we are saying, "I have no CHOICE!"

> **We live conditioned to think we have little choice in how we run our lives. Because we choose to think we have no choice, then indeed we do not.**

When we succumb to this notion, we instantly restrict ourselves. We cut ourselves off from making our lives the way we would really like to have them. Therefore we are stuck with things the way they are. It is like saying, "I can't do that." There is no way you will accomplish anything while you hold the picture in your mind that you "can't". **This is a law. Instead, affirm: I think I can, I believe I can, I WILL...**

Exercising choice in some areas of our lives might not appear to be in our best interest. In a sense this could be true if the price, or consequences of choosing an alternative to the way we currently do things, is too high.

For instance, if we really hate our work, or the working conditions, we could choose to tell our boss in no uncertain terms what he can do with the job. But would the result be too costly? If we did not have another job to go to, the effect of making that choice could be quite disastrous.

So in a sense it appears that we do not have a choice. Yet, if we allow this type of thinking to dominate our minds, we can become stuck in ways that are not as productive for us as they could be. Even when dealing with clients, or friends, but only if they ask, it is often helpful to assist them to discover that choices do in fact exist.

When doing "Brain Integration", or the seminars associated with this program, we are often able to facilitate participants to appreciate they have more choices than they thought. This helps them come up with new approaches to old problems, fresh ways to deal with existing difficulties.

The power of choice is immense. The realization that we actually can make choices where we previously thought we had no choice, is exciting. By exercising that power of choice, we can change our lives to an amazing extent, almost whenever we choose.

We know that change is almost invariably accompanied by a certain amount of discomfort.

It is not until the pain of staying the way we are becomes too uncomfortable, that most of us are even willing to consider change. When we are hurting enough, we are then prepared to undergo the pain of change that goes with choosing a new path.

Change can be scary, but once the changes are made, we experience a profound sense of relief and a new level of joy in our lives.

ARE WE STUCK OR ARE WE FREE TO CHOOSE?

We do not need to be stuck fast in what we do not want. We can approach life in a centered, balanced way, and choose in a loving way, to look at life, and how to live it. In a sense we are given the gift to choose to start our life again every moment we live.

Assess the cost in emotional and/or monetary terms of making certain decisions. Check all the ramifications of making certain choices. What will the results be? Do we really want that to happen?

Making choices can necessitate changes in our lifestyle. What will others think? Can I afford it? Won't it hurt others? Will it hurt me? Changes are scary, the outcome may not be what we think!

What if it all goes "wrong? Or perhaps even more frightening, what if it goes "right!"?

It is our right to choose our own path, always with consideration for the other people around us, but **certainly** not to the exclusion of taking care of our own needs.

Alternatively, before us is a sort of living death caused by inaction. It seems our habitual approach to everyday life tend to bring us the opposite of what we want.

We frequently seem to miss out on the enjoyable things in life. Our usual patterns of behaviour bring us too much of what we do NOT want!! And although we do not like it, all too often we feel powerless to do anything about it because we think, wrongly, that we have no choice in so many matters. Since we can choose, until the day of we die, we may as well choose to live a healthy fulfilled life. A life filled with dynamic actions that produce happiness and joy. Live each moment by precious moment making conscious deliberate choices.

Being in control of your life this way is as exciting as it is fulfilling and rewarding.

It certainly beats being a couch potato sitting in front of a television, or reading profitless, biased, frequently inaccurate newspaper articles, or reading glitzy magazines. Why fritter away our time and our lives focusing on the dross, when the pure gold is out there for us to mine!

There is a wonderful way to become a better you, by choice.

**Conscious CHOICE is a wonderful way of life.
We can CHOOSE... to CHOOSE!**

We've looked at how lack of self-esteem can hold us back, how reprogramming our minds positively increases self-esteem, and that choice empowers us to take control of our lives.

Next we will look at the need to choose a specific **PURPOSE** for our lives which is unique to us. **Then we need to** select **GOALS** which will take us unerringly towards fulfilling our purpose. **We will learn to** create – 'To-Do **ACTION** lists . . . **All this** will start to rebuild our self-esteem, and take us step by step towards Success, Wealth, Health, and Happiness.

CHAPTER TWO

PERSONAL DEVELOPMENT - THE KEY TO THE GOOD LIFE

We are going to look at four things in this section.

1. The need to accept the challenge and the pain of making changes.
2. The importance of having a specific purpose clearly in our minds.
3. How to set goals to reach that aim.
4. The practical action steps we need to take to get there.

FIRSTLY: THE KEY TO PERSONAL DEVELOPMENT IS CHANGE

Most people do not change very much during their adulthood. Perhaps because nobody ever showed them how to, or why they should. This Life Skills learning program will give you encouragement to make changes. Another reason people do not change is pain. Many have tried changing some things once, and it was too painful. This leads to the true statement being voiced by some observers:

> **"People usually only change when the pain of staying the way they are, appears greater than the pain change will involve."**

Being in pain is not the best reason to make changes in your life. Two people hear a seminar on personal development.

- One leaves the seminar yawning, saying, "I've heard all that before!"

- The other leaves and says, "It is great to hear all those things again, this time I am going to motivate myself to make some changes!"

Jim Rohn, one of the most successful teachers of self development in America, tells of a wise older man he met before he became successful. This helpful, knowledgeable sage, with a few well chosen words, enabled Mr. Rohn to begin his progress from failure to success. He had been expressing the fact that he had not got very far in life.

The wise man asked Mr. Rohn, "How many years have you been working?" "Six years." was the reply. The wise man said, "That's a long time to get nowhere!

And how much money have you saved?" "None!", Mr. Rohn replied.

The wise man said, "If your life is not the way you want it to be, what are the problems stopping you get where you want to go?

Mr. Rohn started to list the reasons he had given so many times before to anyone who would listen. "It is the government, and taxes, and all those unhelpful people in my life, and my bosses have not appreciated me, and the traffic slows me down, and, well, because there just isn't enough time?"

The wise man replied, "There is something you have left out of your list of reasons why you have not succeeded as you would have liked."

"And what is that?" asked Mr. Rohn.

The wise man replied, "YOU!" You are not on the list!

Not everyone is fortunate enough to meet a successful, wealthy, wise individual who is willing to take one under their wing, so to speak. I never did, so I got my information from the wise who had made the information available to others. Even if some wise person did offer help, it would be a rare person who would listen, and act on the wise advice they were being offered. A little timely, well heeded advice from someone who has been there and done it, including the video and the T-shirt, if implemented, can be worth millions. I know!

It is my intention to save those who make good use of this program a lot of grief and wasted time. Life is too short to waste a moment, let alone years, and in my case regrettably, decades. I can assure you that I am now making up for lost time! I am forging ahead, at an age when most people are looking forward to sitting back and taking it easy in retirement.

Many people retire in virtual poverty. They while away their last years, pottering around the house, watching too much TV, and consuming too much tea and biscuits.

I intend to go on learning and growing in knowledge, understanding, wisdom, and reaping the benefits of wealth health and happiness for as long as I am able. The way I take really good care of my health, I hope that is going to be a long, long time. I hope you feel the same way about your life.

Here is a powerful ditty Stephanie Mills mentioned in her introduction:

**"If you always do what you always did,
You will always get what you always got!"**

One definition of insanity is to keep doing the same thing, and expect to get a different result!

Write the following poem on a card, and stick it on your mirror where you look at yourself first thing each morning. Read it out aloud with conviction:

**To have wealth, success, be happy and free,
The key to a much better life - is ME!
For my life any different to be,
I need to start right away, changing me!**

One of the most important secrets of success is introspection. The ability as Robbie Burns the poet said, "Aye the gift to gi'us, to see ourselves as others see us."

If we take a brief moment to plan our day, and a short while reviewing what actually transpired, and learning from that, determining to do better tomorrow is a powerful way to live.

Governments come and go, **and** little if **anything** changes. Taxes go up or down, usually up! They say there is nothing certain except death and taxes. Human nature hasn't changed much in six thousand years of recorded history. Traffic is not going to get better. Bosses will always be bosses. Prices will always go up, and there isn't any more time. We all have the one hundred and sixty-eight hours a week and that's that!

So if we are stuck with all that, and those things are not going to change much, then there is only one thing we are left with to change, **ourselves!** No matter what level of success, or lack of it we have reached, the only way forward is to review how we are doing, and change those things we can see are holding us back.

What things about you are holding you back? Vital factors such as: **Saying,** I can't do this or that… Not having a clear purpose. Not having well-defined goals. Failing to adopt a disciplined approach to your Action To-Do lists. Not, "Having enough time!"

"Round Tuits" are always in short supply.
Everyone you ask hasn't got any "Round Tuits".

Ask them! Have you done so-and-so? "No, I haven't got "A Round Tuit" yet." By the time they do get one, the moment will probably be over. (We'll talk about time and procrastination in chapter four.)

Our job, as really progressive live-wires is to change our approach and get "A Round Tuit" **NOW, TODAY, THIS WEEK,** and **THIS MONTH.** The interesting thing is that the more "Round Tuits" you manage to find and use, the happier and the more successful you become.

"Successful" is not something you get, it is something you become. The only way things are going to get better for you is to make yourself better. Better at what you do. Better at your job. Better at being a nice person. Better at being friendly. This program will give you some powerful tools to help you to achieve this.

SECONDLY: TAKE A LONG-TERM OVERVIEW OF YOUR LIFE

When we are young we think we will live for ever, that is if we think about it at all. As the years go by, most of us spend our entire days being caught up with all the detail of day to day living. We rarely think about our lives very far in advance.

We think perhaps as far as to the summer holidays or maybe getting married in next year, or planning to buy a house in a few year's time. In all probability, nobody ever suggested to you that you might start thinking now about the direction you want your next forty, fifty or sixty years to go. Not one person ever helped me to think about it. I wonder why not? Perhaps it is because so few people ever take the time to consider or think about what they really want to achieve in their seven, eight or nine decades of life.

Most people nowadays live well into their seventies, eighties and even nineties. Each decade zips by! The first two you don't know what life is all about. You're preoccupied with so many new experiences: Going to new schools. Meeting new people. Perhaps traveling to different places. Your whole attention is taken up, simply adjusting to being on this earth, and living this highly complex life we lead.

The next two decades: Twenty to forty – you are busy developing a career getting married, having children, and making your way in the world. Or perhaps you have decided to live alone, and concentrate on your job. You've never done any of this before, so it is a constant learning situation. Every moment is taken up just doing all the things that living requires us to do. Then from forty to sixty, the children are growing up. You are hopefully making ends meet, just. Or, you may even be doing rather well financially during those years. Then suddenly, it is time to retire! Life without a salary can be a great shock to those who have no substantial savings. (More on that later in chapter six.)

Then what? You have another two or three decades of life left, but what to do with them? How to spend them? The chances are your health is declining, because regrettably you did not take a long term view of your health, and how best to take care of it. Very, very few people do. Yet there is more information available today about how to attain and maintain good health than in any previous generation. That is why there is a chapter on Health in this book. So if you are determined to make the best of your life, live in the now moment, and whatever decade you are currently in, stop and take stock. This may not be easy! A lot of people worry about death. It is the one thing everyone has to do, no option. To hide from that reality when we are young, or failing to face the fact that we do get older, and die, is a grave error. (Excuse the unintended pun.)

We need to make a careful appraisal of our lives. Examine how we are doing in relation to the way we really want to perform. Once we can see where improvement is desirable, we can start to tackle the job of making changes in our usual way of doing things for the better.

THIRDLY. THE HABIT OF DAILY PERSONAL GROWTH & DEVELOPMENT.

I can now see clearly where I went seriously wrong for over three decades. I studied books and tapes on personal and business development, attended seminars, but did not put the things I read and heard into action on a daily basis.

> **I was always going to get started
> on all the changes "tomorrow".
> Does that sound all too familiar?**

Some say that all good diets begin tomorrow! Or "Jam yesterday, jam tomorrow, but NEVER jam today!" I did begin to do some things, but in fits and starts. Then I just forgot to continue with them as other things crowded them out. Does that strike any chords with you? I hope not, but whoever said that, "The pathway to hell is paved with good intentions." Was only too right, in spades!! So please, why not learn from my mistakes?

**If you get an "Aha", that means if a new concept
or an idea strikes you forcefully,
ACT ON IT RIGHT AWAY!**

Write it down in your organizer, or your notebook or your journal, but write it down. (If you have not yet purchased an organizer, then this might be a good time to make that resolve!) Then when you review the day, week or month, it will jump off the page and smack you in the eye if you have not actioned it!

If you want to learn to play the piano, or any other musical instrument, it does not work to do six hours practice once a month. Fifteen or thirty minutes every day will ensure great progress. Six hours a month is worse than useless. (Fifteen minutes a day is actually seven and a half hours a month!)

To succeed in this life process, we all need a "carrot". If you want to get a donkey to move, donkeys respond to carrots in their field of vision. They also respond to the big stick applied to their rear end! Which would you prefer? For life to whack you one to get you going, or for you to visualize a "carrot" to draw you ever forward??

Choose your own carrot. Is it personal freedom? Is it the accumulation of wealth? Having a wonderful house, a new car? Is it to develop good character? Or to have a positive impact on the world? What do you really WANT? What do you really, really WANT passionately?

Any or all of the above? Identify what it is that you WANT, and you have your carrot or carrots.

For the carrot to work, you have to look at it every day, and really go after it!

**Look for pearls of wisdom every day in every
circumstance, and with everyone you meet.**

I was talking to a check-out girl the other day, engaging her in conversation that took her a little outside the monotony of her job. I was jokingly imitating an impatient child, and stamping my foot, as an assistant took what seemed an age to check something out.

The check-out girl was enjoying the interchange. She looked at me with a mock schoolmistress frown, and said firmly, "O.K. Time out. Go and sit over there, and come back when you are willing to discuss it calmly!" I hooted with laughter, and was delighted with her rejoinder.

As I left the store, I pondered on what the young girl had said. I felt strongly there was a gem in her comment that I could use. I realized that I sometimes take action when I am a bit cross or upset about something.

That command, **"TIME OUT - come back when you can discuss it calmly!"** Will live in my mind, and I will use it to calm myself down for a minute or two before acting. I know that I will make better decisions as a result.

The point I am making is that we can learn from everyone we meet. This is regardless of their age or station in life. If we allow others to be our teacher, we will continuously be adding to our store of wisdom. It is exciting to make learning a habit. There is a sheer joy to be had from taking new ideas on board.

THE THREE SIMPLE STEPS TO SUCCESS –

1. Purpose, 2. Goals, and 3. Action
There are three major but simple concepts which will determine how successful you are. These three will act as a framework for a lifetime of success. They are: Purpose", "Goals" and "Action".

1. **Purpose.** To enrich our joy of living, we need a clear sense of our overall purpose. So, one way to enjoy every day of your life, is to be dedicatedly following your written purpose. Having a clear purpose is essential for anyone who wants to get the most out of life.

2. **Goals.** Create a goal structure to fulfill your purpose. With your purpose in mind, pursue your written goals. They define where you want to get to next. Each goal has its own path that leads to it. To follow that path you need to take practical steps.
3. **Action.** Write out your steps towards goals on "ACTION To-Do" lists.

All the steps to enable you to reach each individual goal are put on "ACTION To-Do" lists. Fulfilling your ACTION To-Do lists is fun because you can see where every action you take is leading.

These three things are the key practical steps to achieve happiness, success and wealth. Let us develop them in more detail.

The 4TH Step: Determining Your Sense of Purpose.

Before you can set goals and chart a course in your life, you first have to have some concept of your overall purpose. What do you want to achieve in life? Riches, fame, notoriety, applause, doing good, helping others to have enriched lives, rearing a family or building a successful business, helping yourself to make the most of your life, good health?

Or all of the above! Probably one of the most important and most satisfying things you will ever do, is to write out your personal purpose in life. It is important that you can actually visualize an umbrella purpose that you can always be working towards. It is important that you feel you can fulfill yourself. You may set lofty goals, and that is excellent, and it is important to be realistic. If your goals are set too high, and are actually unrealistic at this time, then this will hamper your development. If you do not set high enough goals, and have a lofty purpose, then you will limit yourself. The line is fine. Each has to find it for themselves. Want to be an astronaut? Well, that will take some doing. There will be many stages to go through to attain such a rare goal. You will probably not find it the easiest thing you have ever done. It is not easy, and yet it is incredibly worthwhile. First decide what aspects of life are the most important to you internally. What do you need at the core of your being to feel that you have a purpose worth pursuing?

Here are a few suggestions for thought trains:

My Purpose is:
- To develop myself to be the finest individual of which I am capable, by learning, studying and actively practicing the values I learn, and becoming successful in business. or
- To pursue the finest moral and spiritual values, and live my life and practice their application as well as I am able, and develop my interest in the arts and become successful as a or
- To develop fine upright character, as an honest, sincere, kindly person, who continues to grow in wisdom all through my life, so that I can be in a position better to build a wonderful family of children and grandchildren. or
- To expand my mind, my knowledge, and my abilities continuously in order to reach my greatest potential, and excel at my chosen profession. or
- To become wealthy and famous as a... whatever you determine.
- To be the fastest person in the world on foot or in a car.
- To rear a family of successful children who are fulfilled in their lives as well as developing myself to be the best I can be.

As you think about these suggested thoughts, many other ideas will come to you that will be more specific to you. You have your own ideas and plans for yourself. Maybe you could write them down as they come to you. If you carry a notebook and pencil with you at all times, you will find that you get used to writing useful thoughts down. A very valuable habit to develop. The important thing is that you formulate a sentence, or a paragraph of sentences, which embrace everything you want to include in your personal purpose. You may want to change it, or revise it from time to time. Keep your old scripts, it is interesting to compare how your purpose changes in the light of life's experiences.

To be successful in this life, we cannot attain our purpose, or work towards the achieving of our various goals, without interacting with others. Our development as human beings will impact on those around us. The way they react to us will help us to modify our approach as we go along.

This needs an additional amount of thought. How, in pursuing my purpose, can I enrich the lives of others and assist them in attaining their purpose? This might extend your idea of your purpose, to include the way in which you want to impact others.

SOME IDEAS FOR INTERACTION WITH OTHERS
- As I develop as a warm friendly person, and grow wiser, I will be encouraging and helpful to others, being available when asked to help them in any phase of their lives which is uplifting to them.
- My own development will inspire others to work on themselves.
- I want to apply all I learn, and all the character traits I develop, in service to others, to enable them to enjoy their lives and the attaining of their chosen purpose as they allow me to do so.
- I will look for opportunities to learn and glean wisdom from everyone I meet, and from those around me that I love and cherish.

Once you have identified your purpose, or purposes, you can then start to determine your goals effectively, and not before. Of course, if you do modify your purpose at any time, this will necessitate your modifying your goals as well. Goals are subsidiary to purpose. A collection of goals will be constructive steps to help you arrive at your overall purpose.

The 5th Step: Setting Goals

Set yourself some goals. Goals are like destinations. If you do not have any idea of your destination, you are unlikely to reach it!

A little old lady went up to the ticket office in the railway station. "Young man", she called in a shrill voice, "Give me a return ticket." "Certainly madam", said the ticket clerk, "Where to?" The old lady cried, "Why, back here of course, you silly man!" Needless to say, the old lady did not go anywhere that day. Less than 3% of people set out any written goals in their lives. The other 97% either are not aware of any aspect of planned goal setting.

Others don't believe it is necessary, or that it would make any difference if they did. They do not know even if having goals will help. So they don't bother.

No planned destination, no ticket, no journey, no arrival at anywhere worthwhile.

FIRST TAKE STOCK OF YOUR LIFE AS YOU ARE TODAY

Before you start work on your list of goals. Take stock of your life. Give yourself some time to write out a list of all the factors that make you who you are:

    a. What are you good at? What are your natural skills? List them all however small they might seem.
    b. What abilities are you developing?
    c. What do other people say you are good at?
    d. What can you do for others?
    e. What is your current financial position? Make up a list of assets and liabilities.
    f. What do you really enjoy doing?
    g. What really interests you?

Now you have a snapshot of yourself and your abilities written down, you might want to begin considering your goals.

Here is a list of areas of life which might stimulate you when you are doing your brainstorming. Considering these areas, they may prompt you to include more things in your list of goals. There are seven areas you might want to look at:

1. **You. What you want to achieve in life.**
   The things you want to own, to do. The places you want to go. What dreams do you have about what you would like to become? What projects would you like to undertake? What ideas do you have that you have never really pursued, but would like to do one day? Everything that will contribute to your overall purpose.
2. Your partner, or your wife or husband. What do you want to include on your list of goals regarding them?
3. Your immediate family, and your friends. How would you like to change your relationships for the better?
4. Your work. How you can progress at work. What sort of work would you really like to be involved with? What goals do you have concerning your job, or your business?
5. Your finances. How would you like to see yourself in future? Is it your goal to become financially independent? Have you an overall savings plan? Investments for the future?
6. Your future. Think about what you would like to achieve this week, then this month, then this year, three, five or ten years or even more years in advance.
7. Your spiritual development. If all our goals are physical, and relate to material things, we will become spiritually impoverished. Our spirits need nourishing as do our bodies. In the section on happiness, we cover some of the ways we can work in a positive way on our spiritual growth.

Now you have a list to prompt you, maybe you can make a start on selecting your goals. It is exciting to plan what you want to achieve to get the most out of life. Maybe you could begin today.

One way to start your goal-setting plans is to have a brainstorming session. To do this, list as many things that you can think of that you want to have, to do, to be, to see, to go to, to own, to achieve, to build. See if you can make it up to a list of fifty or more things.

The next step is to revue those things that you have written, and check how many of them are consistent with your overall purpose. Any that might deflect you badly might best be put on hold for now until such time as they might be more appropriate.

Then go through the list again, and put a 1 against those that you think you might be able to achieve this year. Then put a 3 and a 5 and a 10 against those things you feel you might be able to achieve in one, five or ten year's time.

Next, if you select from your list and write out ten things you really, really want to achieve this year, date the note, and look at it every day, you will be amazed to watch those things happen if you want them badly enough.

It might be a good idea to priorities those ten in order of importance to you. Then you can apply your efforts to each goal in the order that merits it.

This does not mean that you abandon the others on your list that had a 1 by them. It is just that they will take lesser priority. You may want to add them to your list of ten as some of them become achievements rather than goals. When you re-write your lists, keep the old ones that you have partially completed.

Occasionally you can look back at your old lists, and review what you have done, and what you haven't done. This will give you a clear idea of where you have been, and what you have achieved so far. This will add to your sense of achievement. It will help you with your forward planning. How to do what better, and when.

Your prioritized list of goals can then be expanded, and the practical steps to reach them itemized. So what seems to work well is to put those ten most important goals on ten separate pieces of paper, writing the heading of the goal in capitals, possibly in a color at the top of each sheet.

The 6th Step: Now To Create Your "Action" Lists

Then the challenge is to write out the practical steps you will need to take in order to attain each of those goals. An ACTION "To Do" list if you will. Each item on the "ACTION" list, when accomplished, will bring you a step nearer each of your goals.

Each goal will have its own ACTION list. On occasions they may overlap with other ACTION steps for related goals. It will be necessary to review each list on a regular basis and re-write them deleting those things which have been completed and adding others which have had to have been added. Then whichever goal you intend to work on, you will find yourself looking at the ACTION list, and modifying it from time to time.

As you cross off items and add more to-do action steps, this will give you a sense of progress and accomplishment.

So there we have a plan. This is what we have covered in this section:

1. Recognise that personal development through self-discipline and application is the key to the good life, and everything we can want.
2. When we take a long-term view of life, we get things into better perspective, and are better able to plan for what we want.
3. Our purpose is not so much a destination as a journey. To get anywhere in life we need to know where we want to get to.
4. Our goals are stages along the way in life's journey, that are arrived at as we achieve our clearly defined goals.
5. Action ensures our goals are achieved by steadily performing the tasks needed to get them done.

In the next section we will look at some of the practical ways we can work to realize our dreams using these six key approaches.

CHAPTER THREE

PRACTICAL STEPS TOWARDS ACHIEVING THE SUCCESS YOU DESIRE

Are you running your life? Or is your life running you? This program is all about you taking over more control of your life. Instead of life's circumstances buffeting you around like a hapless piece of flotsam in the waves of the sea, how about getting your feet rooted on the shore, and start making things happen instead.

In section one, we looked at the need to rebuild our self-esteem. Building our confidence is assisted by changing the way we talk to ourselves. We can choose to speak to ourselves in positive, reinforcing ways that raise our self-esteem. When we identify our real purpose, decide on specific goals that will propel us on our way, and implement the steps towards those goals with ACTION To- Do lists, this will also build our sense of self-worth.

**Each achievement, whether little or large,
will support our desire for personal development,
which will provide the fuel for further endeavour.**

It pays to fight off the temptation to fall back into old habits that consume our time, like the TV, and other things that will not help us forward. We need to rekindle the desire to learn and grow. To develop the mind with new information. To stimulate the brain with exciting activity.

We need to face the fact that there may well be times when we feel discouraged.

We might feel that we are not really making much progress. It is not unusual to feel a little depressed sometimes when we are working so hard on ourselves to improve the situation, and so little appears to be changing.

This is where **FAITH** comes in.

We need to have the **FAITH** that every tiny step we take **IS** building something worthwhile. If we could always see immediate benefits, we would not need FAITH. You don't need FAITH that buses run when you see one coming. Faith is having the strength to maintain a clear vision of the reality of something that has not yet happened. So hang in there, and trust that every scrap of effort you are putting into building the "New You" is doing just that.

Whether we are in employment, or starting our own business, or expanding an existing organization, one major key to success is the constant search for new approaches and fresh ways to do things. It pays to keep extending our understanding, especially in this so rapidly changing world. So read, learn, take more seminars, get more personal development programs, and keep growing. Now let us look at seven factors that will help you achieve your aims, purposes, and life goals, and implement your **ACTION** plans:

First: You need a strong desire as fuel for your success engine.
Second: Have a written action plan.
Third: Work your plan, do not deviate from it.
Fourth: Keep a log, journal or organizer with written records.
Fifth: Getting started on track each day.
Sixth: Work smarter not harder.
Seventh: The power of review.

1. IT IS STRONG DESIRE THAT FUELS YOUR DRIVE FOR SUCCESS

The emotion of desire is the fuel that enables human beings to pursue the drive to achieve. The stronger the desire, the more likely you are to achieve what you want.

Successful people recommend we examine ourselves for what we most desire in life.

Then we can write that down as a goal. We sometimes get caught in entertaining ideas of our desires being beyond us, or unattainable. That is something to banish from your mind.

One way to accelerate the power of using emotion to achieve your goals is to transmute emotional power. This means that the energy we would normally waste in negative emotions, like anger, jealousy, greed, envy, we can with practice, transform into positive emotional energy.

This is literally like turning a waste product into a very powerful, viable energy source. Sublimating and transposing any powerful destructive emotions in this way saves wasting energy. Producing a list of what you really, really want to get out of life is fun. It does not matter how preposterous it might seem at the time you are writing it. Everything on that list has to be something you desire. Each item has to be something you can feel passionate about. If you expect to get more of what you want in this life, you have to want more.

However, all this intense effort has to be controlled by moral and ethical constraints. Being greedy and self-seeking, dishonest and double-dealing, destroys character, is not so clever, and will backfire on anyone who practices them in the long run. Honesty, integrity, faithfulness, straight dealing, fair-mindedness are the backbones of fine character

Then knowing what you want, visualize it so strongly, that you can almost taste it!

This is a powerful way to motivate yourself. See what you want in your mind's eye, and feel the excitement that you will experience when you achieve it. See it in the context of your business or professional life. The more clearly you can see it and feel it, the sooner it will come to pass. Working towards your goals transposing emotions in this way is smart. There is an old proverb, "Be careful what you set your heart on, for you will surely achieve it".

The more you desire and really want something, the more likely it is that you will bring it into your life. So it is vital, that what we focus on is a good concept, and that it will have a positive impact on our lives. Yet desire is not enough on its own. Desire is the fuel. It is like the fuel in the tank of your car. It is great to have that full tank of fuel. However, that fuel is only a potential source of energy. In order to use it, you have to fire up the engine and go places with a purpose. Then the fuel is being used to good effect.

In the same way, wanting something passionately is not enough. It is necessary to use the fuel of that emotional desire energy to get things done. It is also vital to have to have a detailed plan of action of how you are going to attain your goal. It is foolish to just put your foot on the accelerator in the car and go fast without direction. You have to steer that power in a right direction, or you crash. It is the same with the powerful emotion of desire. It has to be controlled, directed, and steered in the right direction. And, if you are going on a journey of any length, a written route of the directions, and the roads you will take to get to your destination helps a great deal to avoid driving around in circles, and saves a lot of time.

2. FAN THE FLAMES OF DESIRE WITH ACTION

Thoughts create feelings. Feelings create emotions. Emotions create the motions of change. So if you want to change the way you feel, it is necessary to change the way you are thinking. The five main desire factors are:

Interest. Excitement. Enthusiasm. Inspiration. Elation. Provocation

Sometimes we can provoke one another in a right way to improve ourselves and do better!

Check these four things:

1. Pinpoint what your motivation is. Analyze what it is you want and why you want it. Then work on that reason for doing something, and motivate yourself. Nobody can be a motivator for anyone else. We can, perhaps, inspire someone, give them information, show them another way, but we cannot motivate them. Everyone has to be responsible for motivating themselves.
2. Evaluate your current position in terms of experience, values, education, resources, money, job, environment and locality. See where you are, and get excited inside yourself about where you want to get to. Look at examples, keep beautiful pictures of your dream, where you can look at them regularly.
3. Take what you have presently towards your goals and cause it to grow daily. Watch the growth, and focus on where you want to finish up. **Feel the elation.** Experience the excitement of nearing your goal step by step. This can bring a tingle to your day, expectation to your planning, and joy as you **ACTION** each step on your list. The thrill of achievement is heady stuff. Enjoy it!
4. Mental projections can raise your financial consciousness. Repeat often:

"I have all the money in my pocket, bank account or available to me from savings or from credit that I want. It is ready and waiting for me to use it at the appropriate time."

Here are eight bullet points to speed your progress:
- Study deeply the object of your fired up interest.
- Develop the abilities you will need to progress in this field.
- Use a dictionary and thesaurus to expand your vocabulary on the subject. This broadens the mind. The more words you know, the more effectively and broadly you can think.

- Make a list of all possible opportunities for increasing and broadening your experience, in finances, health, values, and your spirit no matter how obvious or way out they might seem to be.
- Make it a personal goal to read a book a week on a subject that interests you. Choose one that you can get excited about.
- Read all the advertising in trade papers that are related to your projects. Companies spend millions on advertising. The way they present their products is intended to inspire you to want to have what they have to sell. So the pictures, and the words are there, very carefully chosen, to entice you to buy and own. Get as much mileage out of looking at the adverts that exemplify any part of your goal.
- Improve your ability to express yourself on your feet. A course in public speaking will change your life for the better. Afraid of standing up in front of people? That can be fixed in two minutes with kinesiology. You don't believe me? Take me up on it, try it. We have seen it happen over and over again. We love to see someone who, one minute is totally tongue tied, and red with embarrassment at the thought of speaking to a group, the next minute relaxed and happily enjoying the experience of sharing something of themselves with a small audience.
- Find out where people are going and take them there. If we watch for trends, and observe what people are interested in, it is possible to "catch the wave" so to speak. The public at large has fads and fancies. One minute we see someone with a hula-hoop, then suddenly everyone seems to own a hula-hoop. If we can see a fad coming and get in on the action, it might be an opportunity for real increase.

2. HAVE A WRITTEN PLAN - AN ACTION LIST

You may have heard, possibly too many times: **"If you fail to plan, you plan to fail."** Whatever you do, do not let this golden rule become boring old hat to you. It is a most valuable proverb. Use a daily, weekly, monthly, and yearly written plan. A three ring organizer greatly helps with this job. Each longer term list will probably be less detailed, but nevertheless will form your framework for action.

Just formulating these sheets of paper takes planning, and some real thinking time. There is great value in having a written plan. If you are truly expanding your mind, you cannot keep everything in your head. I know, I've tried, and it nearly drove me nuts.

Have you ever tried to keep directions in your head that someone is giving you in the car? By the time you are up the hill, and you get to the cross roads, you're saying to yourself, "Did he say left at the first junction or the second?" If you have a map, and you write down directions, it takes all the strain out of it. So with everything!

3. WORK YOUR PLAN

Here is another golden oldie adage. It is one you will never regret using: **"Plan your work, and work your plan"**.

This phrase, like the previous one described at 2. Above, are extremely valuable truisms. They can make the difference between your great success and your miserable failure. They apply to almost anything we do.

The trouble with pure platinum sayings like this is, that we hear them maybe in the wrong context for us and we say, "Oh Yeah! How many times have I heard that one." That is not a profitable reaction. It is negative and destructive. Instead, get mileage out of it! Use it for your benefit!!

If you have your written set of goals, and you have written out your To-Do lists, you have a plan.

Now "Work Your Plan!"

Let's take something really trivial. You write a shopping list out. You even add one or two last minute items. You go off to the supermarket, and when you get there you find you have left your list at home! Did that ever happen to you? No! Of course not. But I am telling you that it has happened to me. And more than once. So I do all my shopping, doing my best to remember all the things on the list. When I get home, I have forgotten the one thing I really needed. It was on the top of the list, underlined too! The butter. I forgot the butter!! Then I realize that I bought several things that were not on my list. And yes, you've guessed it, they were things I did not really need or want.

So what was the problem with this little shopping expedition? I "Planned my work", but I did not "Work my plan." So to an extent, I failed satisfactorily to achieve my entire goal.

I deliberately chose something really trivial, yet you know how annoying and energy wasting such an event can be. (That is of course if it has ever happened to you. If it has not, something else like it has, I'll bet my boots.) So if it is upsetting (don't forget to sublimate!) and time wasting with such a tiny issue, what about your major goals in life?

What about your vital To-Lists that will take you to your goal? If you do not write them out, you cannot follow a plan you have not made in writing. It pays to be orderly. To be in control of your life feels wonderful. When we do things in a planned and systematic way, it is pure joy.

There is still plenty of room for spontaneity. I am not talking about becoming an organized robot following the plan every second of every day! There is plenty of opportunity to forget plans, and just chill out, if that is what you planned to do!! (Sorry about that!!)

Go-getters allocate some time each day, first thing in the morning and last thing at night, for planning their work. If you have not been used to making written lists of goals, plans, and things you want to achieve, perhaps you might start today. It takes all the strain off the brain, so long as you remember to keep them with you.

This is time more than well spent. This is diamond time. This is when you are preparing to dig out the nuggets that will form your gold bricks!

Some people use "organizers", and these are great so long as you do not become a slave to it. They can lock you into your left brain if you are not careful. Time managing systems make fantastic servants, and poor masters. You can get caught in the trap of spending more time organizing your life than you spend living. This is unlikely for the majority, considering 97% of the population never plans anything more sinister or exciting than a shopping list!

4. "KEEP A LOG OR JOURNAL OF ALL YOUR WORK ON GOALS."

Keeping a journal of the steps you took to get from here to there or from a) to b) might be revealing and helpful. You may not actually follow the "ACTION" list exactly, because circumstances alter cases. As we go along, it is vital to stay flexible in our approach. If you keep some form of journal each day, it helps to see written down the sequence of events and what we did when. This does not have to be lengthy. Far from it. The more succinct it is the better. You only need enough information to jog your memory when you look at it later.

This vital piece of information about journals or logs should also be on a note attached to every new computer in large capital letters in red, so that newcomers to computers know to do it to start with. When I was writing my first textbook, I was working with hundreds of files on my computer. For a while, I could keep track of what was in each file in my head. I soon found that I could not always remember the name of the file. So I would start looking for it. Sometimes I would spend all morning searching for one file. Often it would have been quicker to write it again!

Sometimes I found the file I was looking for, sometimes I did not. The frustration was incredible and very wasteful of nervous energy. I then decided to keep a log of every file I ever created in a spiral notebook. "Obvious!", do I hear you say? Are you thinking, "I can't believe you didn't do that to start with."? Well, it may be obvious to you, but I did not do it. I know now that I should have done, but that is hindsight. You know that hindsight is 20-20 perfect vision, I'm sure. So learn from my mistake, and keep a log. Also a journal, it is useful to be able to see when you did what, when you met whom, or when you bought…

5. GETTING STARTED EACH DAY

Some people say, look at your list, then pick the thing you want to do least and do it first. Maybe that is a good idea for you. Maybe that will be the best thing to do sometimes. This is especially true if you wake up with good energy, raring to go.

Perhaps it would not be such a good idea if you are the type of person that takes time to get going in the morning. Those who tend to be rather slow starters, might be better employed at the beginning of the day doing something they know they can do easily and well, and tackle more difficult tasks later. But it is a choice you can decide to make.

Completing a task or two rapidly in the beginning of the day, makes anyone feel better. It brings an immediate sense of joy and satisfaction.

Successful completion of tasks generates energy, and a desire to achieve more. Perhaps, having accomplished something, or after a few cheering successes, then might be the time to tackle the nasty difficult job. You know yourself, you don't need to let others plan how you work best.

6. WORK SMARTER NOT HARDER

Another overused slick phrase, that should not be seen as a slick phrase at all is, "Work smarter, not harder." We can learn what works for us. We can learn what gets most done in the shortest time the way we work. It is exciting to find new ways of doing old things. Often, the really smart way to work is to get someone else to do it while you get on with something even more productive.

When you analyze what is the most cost effective way to do your stuff, you will still work hard, but because you're working smarter you will achieve more and more. "Hard work never killed anyone." Or so the saying goes. But I would say that slogging away, working harder at hard work which is not really productive or fulfilling, working under tension and stress has brought on the heart attack that has killed many a zealous worker. So I would prefer to say, "Smart work never killed anyone." Smart work just brings greater success!".

7. THE POWER OF REVIEW

It is comforting to spend a little time each day reviewing what you did, your progress and revising your lists. A good time to do this review is in the evening for a few minutes, preferably just before you go to bed. This might be a good time to review or fill in your log or journal. Then check what you did against the **ACTION** list you started the day, week, or month with.

If you feel a little unhappy about the way the day went, in that you did not achieve all you set out to, be kind to yourself. You did do your best, didn't you. Yes? Then be happy with yourself. It is counter productive to be overly critical of yourself. Treat yourself gently, and plan how you will do even better tomorrow is a much better approach. Similarly, it is best to be gentle and forgiving with other people as well. We all do our best, and we all get it wrong from time to time. Being merciful to ourselves and others is an up-building character activity.

You may decide to spend a little while analyzing any failures you may have had, and do your best to detect where you went wrong. If you can genuinely see that you could have performed better, work out how. Making notes helps. One way to find forgiveness for yourself, is to plan carefully, follow the plan the next day, get it right and be more fulfilled. Result? Happiness.

≈ SUCCESS ≈

This method of reviewing the day is a policy adopted by many of the people in the top echelons of commerce. That is how they got to be at the top!

It is the practice of some of the most successful people in the business world. They will tell you that review is one of the secrets of their success.

Then when you go to bed, if you have any quandaries on your mind, there is a simple, yet effective technique you might like to try. Sit on your bed, while you are thinking about the problems you want to solve, sip from a full glass of water. Sip and think until you have drunk half the glass. Then put it down and go to sleep.

In the morning, the first thing you do is to put your feet on the floor, and sip the second half of the glass of water. As you wake up in the morning in this way, you may find your problems solved, or new ideas will come to you. Such is the power of the subconscious mind.

Focus on RELAXATION, MEDITATION, AND REVIEW. Another way to handle the end of the day, is to undertake some contemplative review in a state of deeper than usual relaxation works wonders when you have been stressed. Some form of meditative relaxation might help you to keep things in proportion and in priority. When we are thinking hard the brain is working at 14-21 cycles a second, these are called beta waves.

When we are in a contemplative, dreamy state of relaxation our brainwaves slow down to 7-14 cycles a second. This 7-14 frequency is called alpha waves. One way to induce alpha waves is by adopting a comfortable position where you will not be disturbed for a few minutes.

Breathe slowly and deeply. Then focus on each part of the body in turn with your eyes closed starting with the toes and working up the body. Visualize your toes relaxing one by one. Then visualize your calves relaxing, first one side then the other. Then your knees, thighs, hips etc. All the way up your torso an organ at a time.

Finally relax your mind. In this state you are at one of your most creative states of mind. Then bring yourself back to the room you are in, and the circumstances around you and be relaxed and awake.

Then as you go to sleep, enjoy the pleasant sense of looseness and relaxation you are feeling all over your body, and appreciate the way in which your mind has slowed down to a more restful condition. Then when you wake up in the morning, you can look over your day and the things you want to achieve to get you closer to fulfilling your lists. It will give you satisfaction to complete whatever is necessary to accomplish your goals.

Incidentally, the **power of review** also works to an amazing effect when you are learning new material about anything. The trick is to review the notes you took of what you learned the same day you learned it. Then you can review them the next day, put them by and review them again in a week, then a month, after two months, then after three, and so on. In this way you will never lose what you have learned.

So here is some review: With my overall purpose in life clearly defined. I set goals. I need clear focused goals of what I really, really want. Focused goals will become a reality. I have seen this happen over and over again. Write goals and affirmations in the first person singular present tense. Am I drifting along, or do I have discipline, tenacity and intensity of purpose? Change is not easy.

It is definitely worthwhile. The old negative 'going nowhere' crowd will not help me progress. I will associate with positive, growing people.

Make up ACTION To-Do lists, and work them. Visualize my day first thing, when I get up. Using a mini- trampoline or rebounder for even only two or three minutes, will help clear my head and raise my spirits. Set the scene for the day with positive thoughts and affirmations. I will achieve my goals today. I will be successful in all I put my energy into.

If we do not focus on positive ideas, inspirational motivating uplifting books tapes, etc., on a daily basis, we are not serious about personal development or developing our true potential. Feed your mind daily. Tell yourself with conviction:

- "I am growing and developing my mind."
- "I am attracting a perfect partner into my life."
- "I am using my mind to develop ideas to make my business successful."

Or choose your own mental affirmations that lead you to what you want. So in summary and review: Keep FAITH in yourself that you are growing and moving towards the achievement of your purpose. Check over your goals morning and evening, and re-do your ACTION lists.

Fight any feelings of discouragement. Take great pleasure in the things you have achieved, however small. Keep learning, and stimulating your mind. We have looked at seven practical steps to achieve the success, and wealth you want. Here they are again:

1. Recognize that DESIRE is the fuel that gets us started, and gives us the energy to persist until we win. We fan the flames of desire focusing on what we want with passion. Study, learn, and list the values we want to develop and produce, improve our ability to communicate both in the written and the spoken word.
2. Have a WRITTEN plan of action. Make your plan work, follow your plan, and keep a log of what you actually do to encourage you or spur you to continue along the way. Start early doing something you enjoy doing, and will get satisfaction from achieving. Work smarter not harder, and use the POWER of review.
3. Work your plan as you have decided. Keep it free flowing so you can respond to changing circumstances, but stick to your plan.

4. Keep a log or note what actually happens in an organizer, so you have a record of your progress, or lack of it when things did not go according to plan. Cross off the items you complete as you go, that is a very satisfying habit to adopt.
5. Get started on track each day. Take a few minutes for some thought as to where you want to go, what you want to achieve.
6. Work smarter not harder. Use your records to enable you to take short cuts that work, ways that saved you minutes
7. The amazing power of review. Keep a check on yourself. Take an overview of your day each evening, and note what worked for you, and what did not go so well. This way you can to beat the bogeyman next time around.

In the next section, we are going to look at the precious value of our TIME which is our life.

≈ SUCCESS ≈

CHAPTER FOUR

YOUR TIME IS YOUR LIFE - IF I ONLY HAD TIME - OR HOW TO ACHIEVE MORE BY DOING LESS

We all have one hundred and sixty-eight hours a week, yet we hear the familiar cry every day, "I don't have enough time!" This plaintive cry of desperation is a symptom not a problem. It is a symptom of a modern pandemic 'disease' caused by two organisms called "Gotta", and "Rushing". How are "Gotta" and "Rushing" contracted? They evolve slowly, and involve a creeping sort of mental aberration which begins slowly, usually unnoticed, but finally takes over. We can actually be addicted to "gottas" and "rushing"! The "Gotta" bug is the first to get a hold. Items requiring our attention and things we have to do seem to multiply. So we find ourselves saying, "I've "gotta" do this, and I've "gotta" do that, not realizing that we are caught in a trap that is going to end in chronic distress.

As if these self-imposed "gottas" are not bad enough, other people also tell us that we have "gotta". Our spouses, our children, our bosses, our friends all seem to get in on the act. It seems to be continuous. It must be a conspiracy.

"You've "gotta" fix that dripping tap." Says the wife. "You've "gotta" take me to the swings, you promised.", Says one of the kids. "You've "gotta" finish that job tonight.", Says your boss. To crown it all, you just get home and your friend says, "You've "gotta" come to the game tonight." The "gottas" have gotcha!!

When the "gottas" begin to snowball, our normal response is then affected by the second organism called "rushing". The "rushing" soon gets a tighter and tighter grip on our lives. We begin to find that we are rushing from the moment we put our foot on the floor in the morning until we flop exhausted into bed at night.

So how do these two affect the central nervous system? They cause a constant strain on the often already overworked endocrine system, particularly the adrenal glands. Putting ourselves under time pressure, and allowing ourselves to be pressured by others creates mental stress which further overworks our tired adrenal. The mental stress causes a chemical reaction called the "fight/flight" syndrome. Most of the time when we are being pursued by the "gottas", we are also "rushing" in an attempt to fight off the dreadful stress they cause. Or we are suppressing, or giving in to, the desire to flee, fast!

The adrenalin rush caused by this feverish activity is a drug that can get people hooked. It is addictive in the same way that some drugs are. It puts you onto a sort of "high". While that adrenalin is flowing, you feel great. Coffee, caffeine, and smoking all over-stimulate adrenalin activity.

Stress also produces endorphins which have a numbing and painkilling effect, as well as producing a certain amount of euphoria. This can also be addictive. As with other addictions it is not easy to give up. Usually, people do not give up drugs that make them feel good unless it is forced on them one way or another.

If such folks don't keep going, they feel guilty that they are not doing enough. They are pursued by the demon that they should be doing more. If they do take it easy for a brief while, the "gottas" pile up, and when they go back to their tasks they appear to have multiplied. This "proves" to them that they cannot afford to stop.

They may also experience great fatigue if they slow down, or stop working so hard, as the adrenal glands are used to responding to all the stress they create. As soon as the stress levels are reduced, initially there can be a drop in blood sugar, the fuel the body uses for energy. If this type of tiredness is overridden by more and more work, the eventual result can be a type of M.E. long term exhaustion.

Yes, tough minded, go-getters, the achievers of this world, laugh if you mention they may be over-stressed. They say, "I can handle it.", or "I'm fine." But they are not. They do not realize that they are running "low on fuel". They cannot see that the gauge reads "empty", and that they are running on some sort of reserves.

As they whizz about, (Whizz kids?) Rushing from one "gotta" to the next, they do not realize that it is all going to come to a sudden halt one day, eventually, perhaps sooner than they think.

They may fall prey to 'viruses', or some other condition or disease due to their lowered immune system and their poor state of health. They may just get depressed as they attempt to "beat the system" which attempts to regulate body functions. There are laws of health which you cannot flout with impunity.

Another category of "tireless" workers who mostly are in a state of constant exhaustion are the mothers of this modern world. Mothers are frequently pressured into being 'victims' of those they love the most. Often holding down a full or part-time job as well as looking after children, and catering to the needs of a husband, it is any wonder they feel they have "gotta" keep "rushing" or they will never cope.

Our magnificently designed bodies can sustain this fevered activity for quite a while. Strong people can deal with it for years, maybe a decade or two. Weaker people become worn down by it more quickly.

The more exhausted by the "Rushing" virus, the more we are in danger of catching every illness that is "going around."

Or "rotational" viruses as they are puckishly called. Three colds a year, a bout of 'flu, hay fever miseries for a few weeks, and occasional allergies causing fatigue or worse, have become the norm for many.

Talk to most people and they will tell you that they are tired a lot of the time, if not all the time. They have to push themselves, just to keep going. This is a really serious warning signal. If tiredness is not dealt with, if the load is not lifted, the result can be more than tedious, it can be devastating. What sort of result? "Burn-out", "Breakdown", "M.E.", "Post-Viral Syndrome", "Nervous debility" are all names for very similar problems which wreck the health of active intelligent hardworking people. Recovering from these problems can be a long uphill struggle.

If you know that you are in this category, it is imperative to slow down. Take pressure off yourself, and do not allow others to pressure you. "That is all very well," I hear you say, "but if I don't do it, who will?" Maybe so, maybe you are doing an important job, and only you can do it at the moment. Maybe a lot of people rely on you. But if you are in hospital tomorrow, or dead, who will do it then? Either someone else will, or it just won't get done. The world will go on, with or without you, believe it or not! Things will adjust. Nobody is completely indispensable. So why wreck your health? There is a solution. And it takes courage to apply it.

Exercise your greatest power - CHOICE!
"CHOOSE TO DO LESS".

That choice is always open to us. We may not like the imagined consequences of doing less, but whatever the real consequences are, they are not as bad as losing your health. Those awful consequences you imagine will happen from doing less will eventuate if you are too sick to work anyway for any protracted period. So how about making a decision to start doing less today? Yes, today!

Here are some suggestions how you might begin to slow down just a little. Here are several practical ideas for your consideration which might enable you to reduce the "gottas" and begin to take the foot off your "rushing" throttle. Focus on one to start with. Write them into your daily plan.

START TO MOVE AND BREATHE MORE SLOWLY?

Become conscious of how you move. Catch yourself dashing around, and see how quickly you are going. Resolve to take slightly longer paces, and deliberately slow down your gait. Watch and be conscious of how you are breathing. Most people breathe very shallowly. Find out about diaphragmatic breathing and practice it when you are not stressed.

Catch yourself 'rushing'. Take a deep breath, relax your stomach muscles and start walking more slowly towards your destinations, even if it is only for a few yards. You will be pleasantly surprised how much more relaxed you feel both mentally and physically. You will find, as with all habits, that it will take you a while to become a steady mover instead of a dasher. You may frequently get caught up in the mad hectic rush of the life you have previously built for yourself, and find yourself moving quickly again. Be patient with yourself, and remind yourself. After about thirty or thirty-five repetitions, you will begin to move more slowly and deliberately as a matter of course.

PERHAPS BEGIN TO SPEAK MORE SLOWLY?

It appears that everyone on the radio, the TV, and in daily life is speaking more and more quickly. On soaps, the actors seem to leave virtually no pauses between their own lines, and the lines of those they are speaking to. It gives the impression that the actors are rushing through the parts they are playing. It is almost as if they feel that if they do not get the words out fast enough, the house will catch on fire, or they will miss the bus.

Even news readers and weather people on the TV have caught the "rushing" disease, and don't even mention the adverts! Speaking a little more slowly gives you more time to think. More time to collect your thoughts. As you deliberately slow down your delivery, it will encourage you not to jump in when someone is talking to you. It is so much better to wait until the other person has really finished what they want to say.

When you take the time to listen, really listen, it will help the other person feel more relaxed. They will also appreciate that you are really listening to them and taking the time to hear them out. This will be a refreshing change for most people. Have you noticed that we are rarely listened to with careful, patient, undivided attention.

Regrettably there may be occasions we have to interject with some individuals. We have all met the type of person who monologues, and completely dominates the scene. In order to have a conversation one, might have to interrupt.

We might need to say something like, "I'm really interested in what you are saying, and I would like to join in and make it a conversation." This is not a desirable state of affairs, but may be the only way to share information with some people, or to prevent one person from totally dominating the gathering.

DO NOT BE TEMPTED TO OVER-SUBSCRIBE YOUR TIME

It is wise to limit the number of things you take on. This involves being willing to say, "No!" Both to yourself and to others. Be realistic when preparing your ACTION To-Lists to achieve your daily goals. If you do expect too much of yourself, then you are inviting the feeling of disappointment when you do not achieve all you set out to do. It is far better to plan your time conservatively. Then if you do happen to find you have extra time, then you can choose whether to do more things or take a short break.

It is not always easy to limit your list, especially if you are excited about various projects. This is where a certain amount of self-discipline comes in. If we are not running our lives, striving to reach goals, and working towards our overall purpose in an organized but reasonable manner, we will also be in danger of falling prey to the dreaded "gottas".

Give yourself permission to slow down, and to achieve success at a more reasonable speed.

THE APPROVAL TRAP - GIVING AWAY YOUR TIME

Some people find it so hard to bring themselves to say "No!". When other people ask us to do things, do we sometimes say, "Yes", and agree to do some time consuming task, when we should have said, "No!"? If you suffer from this syndrome, a book you may like to read is called, "When I say No, I feel guilty" by Manuel J. Smith, Ph.D.

And guess who the person is they find we hardest to say "No" to? You're right, it is themselves. They have a dreadful case of the "I've gottas". Their own conscience, guilt, driving force, or whatever just won't let them say "No". They want approval of others so they dare not say. "No!"

We also want to please others. Whoever is next on the list you find it hardest to say, "No!" To, only you know. Perhaps it is everyone. In which case you have it badly. But there is hope. You can recover from this pattern. It requires a difficult decision. One where you are able to say, "No, I am not able to take that on at the moment." No apology, no justification, just "No."

ON THE OTHER HAND, WHO CAN YOU GIVE SOME TIME TO?

Sharing your precious time with others is an essential part of expansive personal development. Everyone has something for us to learn from. Whether it be vocabulary, experiences, or know-how, each person we know can enrich our lives. This is not always true, however, if the people with whom we are associating are in a completely negative frame of mind which we are quite unable to balance out.

Have you ever had anyone who outstayed their welcome? You wished they would leave, so that you could get on with the productive things you had decided to do. Maybe they are not as aware of your needs as they might be. One thing to check ourselves on, is are we imposing on the time of others?

PUNCTUALITY: BEING ON TIME IS ONE WAY TO SHOW RESPECT FOR OTHERS

We have covered at length just how valuable time is, whether it is ours or the lives of those with whom we deal. Punctuality in life generally, and for appointments is a matter of courtesy and respect. Although we now have machines, cars and computers that enable us to achieve more than in any previous generation, people seem to have less time.

Everyone is rushing about these days. As the pace of life gets quicker and quicker, everyone seems to be going faster and faster, and for some reason, punctuality seem to be secondary. "I'm sorry I'm late." How often have we heard that cry.

During the blitz of World War II, Mr. Churchill was holding a cabinet meeting in the bunkers under the buildings in Whitehall in London. The meeting had been going on for a while, and a cabinet minister came into the room about half an hour late. He mumbled, "Sorry, the bombing last night blocked the roads, the buses were not running, and there were no taxis. "

Churchill interjected, "Nonsense man, you did not leave home early enough!"

In 1938 Hitler took over the German speaking areas of Czechoslovakia as agreed with Britain's Prime Minister, Mr. Chamberlain. In doing so he gained control of the borders and the security of the whole country. Hitler had agreed that this would be his last territorial gain. But, within days, he summoned the President of Czechoslovakia to a meeting at 7.00 p.m.

The President arrived early, and was told that Herr Hitler would see him in due course. In fact, Hitler was watching movies in his private cinema. Hitler humiliated the Czechoslovakian President by keeping him waiting until 2.00 a.m. when he finished watching the films.

Whenever we (decide to?) keep people waiting, in essence we are showing disrespect to them. We are not appreciating that their time is their life. Every moment of everyone's time is precious. It is not just that "time is money" it is actually worth more than money.

When we are not punctual perhaps we are not appreciating that their time is their life. "I'm sorry I'm late, there was a blockage on the motorway." or "You wouldn't believe the traffic!" are really weak-kneed, pathetic, excuses! Planning to arrive early, and doing so is a sign of good organization and respect for others.

I would like to acknowledge someone for their punctuality. I have never known my colleague, Stephanie Mills, who worked with me for over twenty years, to be late. Despite train strikes, snow, bad weather, she always has arrived early or on time when she traveled to work by public transport. Now she has a car, she never blames the traffic for her early or timely arrival!!

I wish I could make the same claim for myself! She runs her life in such a way that she is early for everything. No excuses. No justification. It is a wonderful thing to work with someone who is so utterly reliable. Incidentally, Stephanie has a high level of respect for people, and is very polite. She believes that it is disrespectful and rude to be late when people are expecting you. So she makes sure she will be on time. She has taught me much in this area.

Of course there may be occasions when events out of our control cause us to be late, but they should be extremely rare. We do not need to be late if we are planning our time effectively.

Why then are people late so much of the time now? Well, either they are attempting to fit too many things into their day, or they are not allowing for contingencies like traffic. It isn't as if traffic comes as a surprise. Everyone knows it is there, every day. So to be late "because of the traffic" is simply a sad statement that we did not use our brains to plan ahead, by taking such delays into account.

Every moment of everyone's time is precious. It is not just that "time is money" it is actually worth more than money. If being late is a trait, then perhaps making punctuality one of your goals might be more than a good idea. Develop a feeling of profound respect for your personal friends and also your business colleagues. Have the type of respectful consideration that drives you to be punctual for them, and for yourself.

**Time cannot be saved - it can only be spent!
That is something to think about!**

MEETING PEOPLE AND CLIENTS - PUNCTUALLY!

Remember another aphorism: **"There is never another opportunity to make a first impression!"** This is a good thing to bear that in mind during the first few moments of your interaction with anyone you are meeting for the first time.

Believe it or not, most people form judgments about the people they meet in the first ten seconds. Then they spend the next thirty seconds justifying what they think about you. If you start your new contact with mumbled apologies for being late, the first impression is sealed.

ALLOW EXTRA TIME FOR THINGS TO GO WRONG

According to the first law of Murphy, if something can go wrong, it probably will. So everything in life does not always go according to plan. The unexpected difficulty does occasionally arise.

If there is no leeway in your packed schedule, when something does go amiss, you will not have the time to deal with it. Either that, or you will immediately be put under unreasonable pressure to get everything you planned to do, done. So wise planning leaves spaces between busy events. If you finish up being early, or having some time to spare, there is always something an active mind can think of to use the time profitably.

BLOCK INTERRUPTIONS

If you need a block of time to accomplish a task, it is necessary to arrange for yourself to have that time uninterrupted. If you work alone, that is relatively easy. It is helpful to choose a time when you are unlikely to have personal callers. Then if you unplug the telephone, you can have a period of productive time without interruptions.

The mobile phone has almost taken over our world. Have we allowed it to intrude into every moment of our lives. We managed without them a few years ago. Yes, of course they are a boon, BUT they can also be like spoilt children, constantly interrupting our lives. They can be turned off, and should be turned off out of consideration for others, let alone for our own peace and productivity.

If you work with other people, or there are others in the house, you will need their understanding and support. I use one ploy to get some clear time. I tell my colleagues and my family that if my office door is shut, it is because I need uninterrupted time. If it is ajar, then they are welcome to call in. This is ongoing and saves the need for daily explanations. If it is impractical to unplug the telephone, ask someone else to answer it and take your calls for the next while. You might tell them, "No exceptions, except emergencies." That way you can set aside a special time to may your return calls.

EACH DAY, FIRST PREPARE YOURSELF FOR THE WORLD
Think calmly. Meditate quietly. Visualize handling things with ease. Use visualization and creative intelligence to select what you do. All effective action is preceded by rest.

CHOOSE WHAT YOU LIKE TO DO BEST
Did I hear you say you can't? To some extent you can, guaranteed. How about pleasing yourself more, and others less. Too many people are heavily into sacrifice. They need to sacrifice less and enjoy their lives more. Others are into exploitation. You really do not need to allow them to exploit you! When you set attainable, reasonable goals that you can achieve you bring joy into your life as you achieve them. Setting too many lofty goals will produce stress and a sense of failure.

It is said, "If at first you don't succeed, then try, try, try again." That is OK, and wonderful to have that type of persistence. It is also wise to know when you are wasting time on getting nowhere with something. So…

If at first you don't succeed, give up and do something you are better at!

Some find this outrageous. Aren't you supposed to give EVERYTHING our best shot? Of course, but we cannot be brilliant at everything. If something is not your strong suit, delegate it to someone else.

KNOW WHAT TIME YOU DO WHAT BEST

We are biologically different types. There are early birds, night hawks and everything in between. Work out which you are, and plan your work accordingly.

WHERE DO YOU DO WHAT WORK BEST?

Do you have a place, orderly, not messy. Some places are conducive to doing some jobs, other places are more suitable for other work.

CATEGORISE AND PRIORITIZE TASKS

If all the varied and different tasks we want to achieve in order to reach our goals are haphazardly arranged, we will probably not make the best use of our time.

TIME IS YOUR MOST VALUABLE ASSET

If you say you don't have time, that implants negative vibrations into your subconscious mind about how you view time. Having feelings of being "busy" or "tied up" constantly will feed the impression into your mind that you are pressed for time.

You have your whole life to spend as you choose, unless you have made choices that prevent you from choosing right now! But you can even change those things, if you really want to.

When we appreciate that our lives consist of a series of moments which will one day end, it places a different value of each of those moments.

PROCRASTINATION IS THE THIEF OF TIME.

Putting things off is a highly destructive habit. How many times do we spend ages thinking about doing something, avoiding doing it, talking about it, finding other things to do? If we had just done it we would have felt marvellous? Deciding to act now, is a decision which reduces stress. Getting things done releases energy to do more.

WE NEED TO ARRANGE TO HAVE TIME FOR OTHERS

Are the people you want to talk to always "in a meeting", "out to lunch", "busy", or "tied up"? Do we do this to others? Be available.

LIVE IN THE PRESENT

If you eavesdrop on other people's conversations, or watch soaps, you will notice that "u-sta" forms a major part of many people's chatter. You hear them say constantly, we "u-sta" do this, and we "u-sta" do that. We always "u-sta" do… this or that. Or 'Remember we "u-sta" go there…This is called **"Past-ing"** Spending the precious **present** reliving the past is fun in small doses, but all the time?

Is there anything wrong with reminiscing? Of course not! It can bring back wonderful and enjoyable memories. But if the past dominates our consciousness most of the time, we are not taking advantage of the **"NOW MOMENT"**

It is also possible to spend too much time **"Future-ing"** Dreaming of what 'might be'. Or spending hours in talking about what we might do sometime. Does that mean planning for the future is not something to spend time on? On the contrary, it is absolutely essential to plan, as we have covered in detail in this program. It is best to strive for "balance" in all things. Here is a very lovely, short, but powerful poem, given to me by a student in one of my classes:

> **The past is history,**
> **The future's a mystery.**
> **"Now" is a precious gift…**
> **That's why it is called "The Present".**

It is a great gift, or a trait to be developed to be able to keep one's mind 97% on "The Present", with perhaps 1% of our time looking back over how we did, and 2% looking forward to work out how we can plan a better life, and achieve greater wealth, health, and happiness.

If we spend 1% of our time in **review,** that would be 1.68 hours each week. If we take 2% of our time to plan a better life, decide on what things to do and achieve, how to further our goals, we would spend about 3.36 hours a week planning our future in detail. Do we set aside at least some time to do review and plan? Few do! This is a really powerful way to invest some of our time.

Being "in the NOW" relishing and appreciating that we are in the "NOW MOMENT" is exciting, and not at all easy to do on an ongoing basis. Everything we are involved with becomes more three dimensional, more colorful, and in sharper focus.

TAKE TIME TO APPRECIATE AND ENJOY THE "NOW MOMENTS"

Savour the magic moments. "Rushing" and "Gottas" deny us the great joy which can be derived from timely appreciation and reflection.

Gaze for a few moments at the majestic mountains, or the unbelievable engineering of a spider's web sprinkled with sparkling dew, and highlighted in the morning sunlight.

Listen to the crashing of the wondrous waves on the shore for a moment, reflect how they are pulled in and out by the mysterious forces of the pale moon still hung on the dawn sky. Listen in depth to the melodious and harmonic tones of your favorite music.

WE ALL NEED "DOWN TIME" - AND TIME FOR OURSELVES

Spending a little time doing things we don't absolutely "gotta" do, can be very restorative. A walk in the woods, or around the park for a few minutes, or perhaps we might just stand outside the back door for a moment or two, and enjoy the change.

Art, music, theatre, the cinema, reading books that uplift and feed the mind, will all act as a balm and a salve for the brain.

Taking time to daydream about what you would really like to spend your time and energy doing is also highly productive. I was punished for 'daydreaming' at school, were you? Yet planned daydreaming is an important skill in increasing creativity. So now we have a more acute awareness of time.

Be aware, "Our time is our life". This is not a rehearsal!

We can beat the "gottas" and root out the tendency to rush. We can choose to do more by doing less as contradictory as that might sound. By speaking and moving more slowly, we can induce a new found sense of peace. By rationing ourselves and not packing too much in, we can enjoy doing things thoroughly and in time.

We can give our time away, we can share it. By being punctual we respect our friends and all with whom we deal. When we reduce the number of interruptions, we can proceed methodically. We can use our time more effectively when we choose when to do what, when we categorize and priorities tasks.

Realizing that procrastination is the thief of time, we can get on and do, and produce values and happiness as a direct result. Not forgetting to give ourselves a breather and take some time to relax and expand our need for pause.

So to summarize: We really can achieve more doing less in a steady non-rushed manner. We "gotta" beat the "gottas"! Hopefully you think it is time to make some changes.

CHOOSING to move more slowly, breathe more slowly, speak more slowly, give ourselves time to think clearly, and allow some time for things to go wrong. Avoid over-subscribing our time, do not allow others to take too much of our time, but be willing to give others our time. Being punctual as a matter of respect to clients, family, and friends. Screening out interruptions, (especially the mobile phone!) knowing when and where to do what's best, categorizing and prioritizing tasks.

Avoid procrastination. Set aside down-time for ourselves to restore our minds and spirits.

Remember, we repeat for emphasis:

**Time cannot be saved - it can only be spent!
Ponder on that for a while!**

Next we are going to look at the vital need to take care of our health.

CHAPTER FIVE

YOUR HEALTH, HAPPINESS, AND PROSPERITY

SAFEGUARD YOUR HEALTH

Supposing you were a millionaire. You could look at your bank statement or your savings account and see all those figures. 1,000,000. Exciting! Wouldn't it be? To have a million! Let us suppose for just a moment, that your health was represented by the figure 1. Take that 1 away from the string of figures that represents a million. What are you left with? Just a string of zeroes, 000,000, six noughts in a row! So what are six zeroes worth? **Nothing!**

> **So the moral of that story is, if you do**
> **not have your health, then all the money**
> **in the world is no good to you.**

It is a well known fact that it is an unfortunate human tendency to fail to appreciate what we have - until it is taken away! Health is taken for granted by most people. Please don't be like the crowd. There are two sorts of people, the health nuts who are always reading about health, studying diet, and spend a lot of time in health food shops. The other sort, the vast majority, who rarely if ever give their health a thought, unless they have a cold or 'flu, or something else goes wrong.

> **Most wait until the symptoms are unbearable,**
> **or serious disease takes hold then they**
> **want an immediate cure without their having**
> **to change the way they live one jot.**

Somewhere in between those two extremes is a middle way. We suggest balance in all things! Regrettably our school systems give more emphasis to learning about history and math, than to the care, feeding, and preserving the workings of our own miraculous bodies.

The young and vigorous especially give little thought to maintaining their health. Even those who are sports oriented, while training and working out, they are not thinking of their long-term health. They may be building strong agile bodies, but they are not usually thinking about their health except as it affects their performance. The idea of being concerned about their health picture ten, twenty, thirty or forty years from now is not in the mind of many young people. In the early part of this program we talked about the need for taking a long-term view of life. In no other sphere of life is it more important to look at how your behave over the entire span of your life than in regard to your health.

The majority of the population who are not interested in sports performance, but are just getting on with their lives, are not thinking about the decades ahead in terms of their health. In fact, the average Mary and John give little thought to how they might attain and maintain better health. They are probably not even aware that it is necessary.

**The average youthful person is not
the least concerned about what
they eat or drink so long as it tastes good.**

The average person is not even unduly concerned about their level of fitness. They have never given much thought to cardiovascular disease which kills more people than cancer. So they eat what they like, drink what they like, smoke or take drugs if they want to, with little or no thought for tomorrow.

The time to take care of your health is NOW! The best defence against disease is radiant good health. No matter what physical age you might be, the time to take an intelligent interest in how your body functions is NOW.

It is incredible to me that children and young adults graduate from school with little or no understanding of how their bodies work. They do not know the location or the function of their vital organs. They know more about the sex life and anatomy of the amoeba than they do about their own liver and pancreas. They have been taught virtually nothing about diet. Most children graduate from state schools in the 21st century who cannot tell which vegetable is celery, parsnip, turnip, beet or sweet potato! This is principally because their teachers in the main know nothing about their bodies, or what is a good diet either!

YOU CAN'T WORK WELL IF YOU DON'T FEEL WELL!
We are not just a brain. Nor are we just a body. The complex nature of the many parts that make up a human being are all inter-related. Affect one part, and you cannot avoid affecting the entire person. If what you are experiencing in the moment is beneficial to any part, then the whole person will be benefited. Even listening to uplifting tapes or reading personal development type material is a health enhancing thing to do. When we listen to, and concentrate on expansive, positive things, we feel better automatically.

If what is occurring at any moment is having a negative effect on any aspect of an individual's life, then the whole person will be reduced in efficiency. Negative effects are cumulative if unresolved. Each harmful thing we do, may in itself perhaps be insignificant. Together, however they can cumulatively add up to a mounting problem. Ignored, eventually such defensive responses can lead to ill health. In a sense we get up in the morning, wash our bodies, hang clothes on them, then off we go in our heads. We hardly give the body a thought so long as it doesn't hurt.

There are five component parts of our holistic selves: Mental, Physical, Chemical, Energy, and our Environment above and below. All parts of our whole persona are inter-related. We cannot affect one part without affecting the whole. If we are bent out of shape mentally, then we are affected chemically, physically, and energetically. Anything that corrects any part of us affects beneficially the whole person.

This diagram represents thewhole person.

We are endowed with the most powerful computer in our world, our MINDS. The MENTAL powers we have are phenomenal. The effect of our MENTAL attitude, and the thoughts that we think affect everything that happens to us. Our attitude and also influences others quite a lot. We can make ourselves sick or well with our MENTAL approach. We can be positive and creative, or negative and destructive with our MENTAL processes, it is our greatest power to choose.

Our "WITS" program addresses the health of the whole person. But focuses on the efficiency of the brain, how to integrate right and left brain, improve memory, and so on. It shows how the functioning of the brain can be dramatically improved by improving the health of the body. See our website at http://www.kinesiology.co.uk for more information.

The way our physical bodies work, the alertness of our minds, and the free flow of energy are dependent upon the CHEMICAL aspect of the body. The air we breathe the water we drink, the food we ingest, the chemicals, the medicines, drugs, and pollutants to which we are exposed all determine how we function.

Our ENERGY, our life force has to be free flowing to allow optimum efficiency, and that is affected by what we think. It is also very much dependent upon what we eat and drink. We live in an electronic world, and are exposed to many types of radiation like never before. These all affect our bodies' natural energy and life-force.

One thing our school curriculum did not deem necessary was to teach us essential knowledge about how our bodies work. We learned all kinds of information about the dates of wars, algebraic equations, and masses of other information we will never use again as long as we live. But the crucially needed knowledge and understanding of how our own bodies work - no!

The Academy of Systematic Kinesiology offers a Foundation Course in natural holistic health care for anyone who wishes to improve their theoretical and practical knowledge of how to enjoy better health and well-being. There is also two year course for anyone with an interest in serving others in the health care profession. Those who want improve their own health, help others, and enter one of the fastest growing service industries can qualify to do so with this course in Applied Kinesiology.

Incidentally, becoming a kinesiology practitioner is one of the most cost effective business opportunities there is in the market. The address of the Academy is given in the resources section. Anyway, back to your health picture. We are going to take a few moments to look at seven aspects of life and health. It would be presumptuous to attempt to give anything but a thumbnail sketch of how to care for your health in this program. There are many books available on every one of these topics. It might be a good idea to seek some out and read them.

Here are seven points for your consideration which cover eating, taking nutritional supplements, drinking fluids, stress, breathing and exercise, rest, relaxation and sleep.

1. EATING FOR HEALTH

Changing to a more healthy diet is not difficult. There are a few simple principles to follow, that's all. We teach the principle of biochemic individuality. That means everyone is different. What is fit for the goose is not sauce for the gander. One man's meat is another man's poison. Note poison, not preference. In these days of increasing problems with food allergies, it is the staple foods that cause most of the problems.

Many foodstuffs in common use give rise to reactions in the body which may initially go unnoticed, or worse still produce adverse symptoms of many and varied kinds. Large numbers of people suffer from 'rheumatism', aches and pains, headaches, catarrh, eczema, rashes, bad breath, digestive disturbances, constipation or diarrhea and many other unfortunate symptoms which they have come to regard as more or less inevitable. They can all be caused and aggravated by eating certain common foods and drinks.

Researchers in Charing Cross Hospital in London listed the following common foods as being involved with migraines. Wheat 78%, Oranges 65%, Eggs 45%, Tea/Coffee 40% Chocolate 37%, Milk 37%, (our tests show 60-70%) Beef 35%, Corn 33%, Cane Sugar 33% (sugar is really not good for anyone), Yeast 33%, Mushrooms 30%, Peas 28%.

Before you say, "Well, I never have a headache, let alone a migraine." Here is the significant point. Long before people get allergic symptoms, which are an immediate discernable reaction, they are often sensitive to one or more foods they eat regularly. In my experience as a practitioner for over twenty years, (now 65) all these staple foods affect an individual in greater degree when the stresses and strains of life reach intolerable levels.

People usually slowly but surely become sensitive to food they eat every day, or those foods which are their favorites, or those they are addicted to. The otherwise seemingly harmless foods then seem to act as the 'last straw' and send the body into a reactive state. Temporary or permanent abstinence immediately brings relief. But that is not the ideal solution. So here are a few guidelines:

a. Avoid manufactured foods as much as possible. Preparing your own food enables you to prepare exactly what you want to eat.
b. Buy foods that will go bad and eat them before they do.
c. Eat some raw food every day, how much varies from individual. Some people handle raw food well, others do not, so plan it for your needs.
d. Microwave ovens may be more of health hazard than people think or realize. Think carefully before using them

daily. Perhaps it is wiser to consider not using them at all. The author does not, and never has.

e. It is useful to find out your ideal weight for your sex, height, and build. Anything over ten pounds more than the ideal weight means that you are overweight. Obesity starts with a few ounces over the ideal, and a habit of eating just a little too much every day.

2. NUTRITIONAL SUPPLEMENTS

Some people say you can get all the nourishment you need out of a normal diet. If this were true, the average person would enjoy robust health and plenty of energy. Unhappily this is not the case. Three colds a year, the odd bout of 'flu, aches and pains and the "tired all the time" syndrome are more often the norm. Analyses of vegetables, for instance, were made before the second world war, and then again after. The percentage drop in available minerals and other nutrients in the average vegetable was startling.

Monoculture, artificial fertilizers, pesticides, the demise of the earthworm, and other factors have served to make modern day foods less nutritious. Anyone who grows their own knows the remarkable difference in the flavour of homegrown fruit and vegetables. To make up for this deficiency in our food, and to ameliorate the effects of high speed lifestyles, we need more than ever to take some nutritional supplements.

Everyone would be better off if they took a gram of vitamin C every day, and more if they smoke. Vitamin B complex supports the brain and the nerves, and helps us cope with stress. Zinc helps our brains function well, and Chromium helps regulate blood sugar which determines our energy levels. Capsicum, otherwise known as Cayenne Pepper may well prove to be a life saver for many people in terms of circulatory disorders. You may want to read, "Left for dead", by Dick Quinn. ISBN 0-9632839-0-1. The information it contains is brilliant and could save or extend your life!

3. IT PAYS TO WATCH WHAT YOU DRINK

The body is about 70% water, Parts of the brain are 85% water! The only way to clean the body effectively is to drink water. Water is the basis of the electrolyte of the body. If the electrolyte is out of balance, all sorts of things do not perform as they should. Energy levels for instance.

So drinking four to six glasses a day of pure unadulterated water, preferably bottled or filtered as the tap water is not as pure as it really needs to be for optimum health. It contains chlorine to kill off undesirable bacteria, but Chlorine is a deadly gas to humans too! Tea, coffee, are best limited to one or two cups a day. Colas are best avoided. They all contain caffeine which over stimulates the adrenals. We covered overstressed adrenal in a previous section.

There is some evidence to suggest that **MODERATE** consumption of alcohol may actually be healthier than total abstinence. However excess alcohol robs the body of B vitamins. So if you drink quite a lot, it pays to take a B complex tablet daily to compensate for this.

4. STRESS IS A KILLER

Do you really want to allow this time bomb to tick away for you? The number one killer is heart disease. Cases are aggravated by stressful jobs and relationships.

Make a substantial effort to reduce the amount of daily stress. You can, by careful planning, and making some hard decisions. Also cut out unsaturated fats and oils, they may prove to be the main cause of heart disease as more about them becomes known. Read the book, "An Introduction to Kinesiology" by this author, from Amazon.com and use the stress release technique it outlines. Also you will benefit greatly from the relaxation and meditation technique suggested in this program.

Also you may like to re-read the part on Relaxation, Meditation and Review covered earlier. Practice that relaxation technique until you can do it easily wherever you may be. If you do practice it for even a few seconds or a minute or two, you can take the stress out of many situations. Probably best not to exceed fifteen minutes a day though.

5. EXERCISING AND BREATHING

Exercise was compulsory at school because even the powers that be understand how crucial it is to health. Before we get into some information about the easiest and most effective exercise program there is, we need to cover a thorny topic. Smoking.

Smoking is Not Good For Your Long-Term Health

Statistics show that the life of a twenty-five year old who smokes forty a day is reduced by 8.3 years. The nicotine level in the brain determines to a degree the behaviors of the smoker. Long term smokers "know" somehow just what level of nicotine levels in the brain are "ideal" for them. If they smoke lower tar they will smoke more cigarettes, and if they smoke high tar, they will smoke fewer.

Nicotine increases the production of neurotransmitters. Nicotine stimulates the electrical activity of the brain which appears to make the smoker more alert, helps the memory and reduces irritability. It also stimulates respiration, blood pressure and sensations of pleasure, reduces appetite and relaxes muscles. All that sounds great! But the cost on the downside is huge.

As soon as the effect of the cigarette has diminished, then the opposite effects swoop in, usually more intensely. The longer the smoker goes without a "fix", the more irritability, anxiety, restlessness, poor concentration, pulse rate, blood pressure, drowsiness, headaches, increased appetite, insomnia, even diarrhea and/or constipation. Maybe dying an agonizing death from lung cancer. Is it worth it? Smokers think so. Non-smokers and ex-smokers do not think so. If you are a smoker, it would pay you to give it some thought. Carbon Monoxide is a colorless, tasteless gas which kills many people in fires very quickly. Smokers inhale it as they smoke. Blood cells love Carbon Monoxide.

They prefer it to Oxygen by a factor of 200x. Carbon monoxide impairs vision, hearing and judgement.

Exercising and Lymph Flow

What is lymph, and why is it important? We have about eight pints of blood circulating in the body. Blood is pumped round the arteries by the heart, carrying oxygen and other nutrients to the body, and flows back into the heart through the veins carrying carbon dioxide, (CO_2), and other waste. Blood does not go everywhere in the body. It is confined to the blood vessels.

There is twice as much lymph in the body than blood, more than two gallons! Lymph does not have a pump like the heart, but relies mostly on the breathing action, and the movement of muscles as we walk, move and exercise to cause it to flow. Lymph feeds and cleans the body.

Lymph carries nutrients to every cell, and helps to remove some of the waste products generated as the body works. Every moment, we are burning fuel in the body. The fuel is glucose. The rate at which it burns is called the metabolic rate. Whenever anything is burned there is always a by-product, one is lactic acid. A build up of lactic acid in muscles can cause aches and pains.

The Rebound Lymph-Pump Exercise

As discussed previously, most people do not get enough physical exercise. A sedentary lifestyle leads to a stagnant lymphatic system. The result is that the body is neither fed, nor cleansed properly. Needed nutrients do not reach the cells which cannot function properly without them.

The brain and the body needs to be well fed and scrupulously clean to function at its best. A few minutes spent each day in ensuring that the flow of lymph is encouraged is time well spent.

How can we do this easily? One of the most useful inventions of the century is the "rebounder".

These mini-trampolines are not suitable for acrobatics, but they do perform a very efficient and vital need for everyone who uses one. They help the body to pump lymph very efficiently. Michele Wilburn helped the author greatly by her example.

Go to www.starbounding.com/44_minitrampolines

The best Rebounders provide more health value per minute than any other form of exercise. Every time the person using the rebounder bounces upwards, the valves in the lymphatic vessels close. As the person comes down on to the mat, the valves in the lymph vessels open and a volume of lymph moves up the body. It goes into the main lymph drainage vessels in the top of the chest. These vessels drain into the blood vessels and the toxins are removed as the blood passes through the kidneys. This pumping action is repeated each time the person jogs or jumps up and down on the mat. But there is no damaging impact as there can be with road jogging. Until a person has used one of these devices on a regular basis for just a few minutes a day, the effects and the value of it cannot be imagined. It can change one's perspective about many aspects of life, and help one to create a very positive attitude. It also seems to stimulate creativity and lateral thinking.

Most exercise machines have a very short life, then they finish up in the garage, or under the stairs, or in the loft. Rebounding can really be fun, and you can watch TV, or better still listen to music and plan or review your day while you get your essential exercise.

The use of a rebounder brings many advantages to the user which are not obtainable from an exercise bike or a rowing machine. The benefits to health are astounding when it is used properly, conservatively, and on a daily basis for even five - ten minutes or so.

Busy executives would be wise to consider developing the habit of using this form of exercise to for brain enhancement and physical fitness. Start gently, but only after consulting your doctor if you have not exercised for some time. One minute only, building gradually up to two or three minutes, just jogging very gently or going up and down will start to work magic in your life.

Much more important to us than mere exercise in this context is its effect on the brain. What benefits does the brain receive? More oxygen, nourishment, and as a result the brain is more alert. Rebounding also improves clarity, speed of thought, and memory. You will feel less negativity, you will be more positive, more creative, more inspired. You'll have better left/right integration. You experience more effective planning, better decision making, and an uplifted attitude to life.

All this, and more can be yours - simply by making the disciplined decision to rebound ten minutes every day, just five minutes in the morning and five minutes in the evening. Haven't time? You would be wise to make time. One way to enhance the value and effectiveness of rebounding is to do it while listening to uplifting music. Something you like listening to will make it more enjoyable. If you can enjoy baroque music, or other classical music with a regular rhythm, you will achieve an additional benefit in brain integration.

If someone already exercises regularly, they might be tempted to feel that they do not need this particular form of exercise. Maybe not, and rebounding is not performed in this context for exercise, that is just a useful spin-off benefit. The reason for using the rebounder is to enhance your brain power, and pump the lymph which feeds and cleans every cell in your body.

We do not know of any other single form of exercise which will be as powerful an aid to your mental vitality as rebounding can be in your life.

Rebounder Health Benefits

You will have more energy, improved circulation. It helps reduce cholesterol levels, exercises the heart muscles, improves the immune system, strengthens and tones muscles, and increases energy and vitality. Rebounding helps burn off excess fat, and weight control when used before meals. It improves physical coordination, balance, relieves tension, improves digestion, and improves elimination through the skin, improves bowel tone and elimination. That is a lot of benefits, just from a few minutes morning and evening!

How To Start

Rebounding is one of the safest forms of exercise there is. However, if you have not been exercising, do have a word with your doctor. Maybe a checkup is advisable. You cannot do yourself any harm if you follow these rules.

Start gently. Watch a clock, and ration yourself to a minute to begin with. It is not even necessary for your feet to leave the mat to start with. Just rock on your toes, or paddy-paw for a few seconds to get used to the feel of it. Then gently and slowly jog on the mat.

Be very careful when you get off the mat, the floor feels quite strangely solid after a workout. After a few sessions, you can increase the time to two minutes, and then to three. Have about ten minutes as a goal to work towards. The author finds the magic period for creativity and mood enhancement is seven minutes, If ever you get tired or too breathless, STOP. The ideal is to rebound only using as much energy as will allow you to carry on a conversation whilst you do it if you wanted to. If the exercise makes you too breathless, slow down.

The secret of success is consistency. Do it every day. If you do miss a day or two, it becomes quite difficult to resume. Inertia takes over. The less you do the less you want to do. A downward spiral. When this happens, start slowly again. Reduce expectations, and be happy with just a few moments on the mat.

Finally, follow the advice given by those who know rebounding, and all the benefits described will be yours for life.

Diaphragmatic Breathing

One of the effects of deep breathing, or belly breathing as a habit is that is purges the body of excess carbon dioxide.

The brain needs oxygen in abundance to function at its optimum. The brain uses over 20% of all the oxygen we inhale. It consumes more proportionately than any other part of the body.

Deep breathing also enhances lymph flow. It is a useful addition to our health program if we make sure we breathe deeply for some time each day. Take the time to learn how to breathe diaphragmatically. It takes a lot of conscious thought and practice to change the way you have always breathed! So practice.

6. REST AND RELAXATION

Every action should be preceded by a period of rest. The heart works, rests, works, rests, works, rests. If it did not the muscles would cramp up and the heart would stop within a minute. That is the way muscles work best, and it is also the best way to run the whole body. When you work some, rest some, then have a breather, you think more clearly and get more done in the long run.

Hobbies and pastimes are great restorers of balance. We need those games of tennis, golf, badminton, table tennis, and we also need the personal social interaction with the other members of the club.

Workaholics often spend too much time alone, and would benefit greatly health wise if they spent more time in the relaxed company of others.

7. SLEEP

Just as with exercise, it seems that the majority of the population gets either too much or too little sleep. Research indicates that between seven and eight hours is about the best average. There is now evidence to support the ancient adage, "Early to bed, early to rise, makes us healthy wealthy and wise." It appears that when the body is put to rest early, the hours of sleep before midnight are more restful than those after.

According to some studies, the hours before midnight are worth twice those after midnight. This is apparently because the effect of the moon on our body fluids and cells is at its height as the moon comes up. We know that the moon's force moves the whole mass of water that constitutes the world's oceans causing tidal action. We are 70% water, so it is not unreasonable to see that it could affect our waters in some mysterious "tidal way" also.

Mattresses have and average life of eight years. Some high quality ones last a lot longer. Check yours to make sure that it still supports your body adequately. If it does not, buy a new one!

TAKE ACTION NOW IF YOU DO NOT FEEL 100% WELL

**Almost any health problem is much more
Easily dealt with in the early stages,
so never put off consulting a health professional.**

If you have problems with fatigue, insomnia, indigestion, constipation, back ache, shoulder pain, or any of the common ailments, you would be wise to visit your doctor for a checkup. When he has given you a clean bill of health, and told you that you do not have any disease that he can diagnose, and then take the next step.

Find the telephone number and the address of your nearest qualified Applied Kinesiology practitioner. There are many "cowboys" who claim to use muscle testing. They may have taken a few weekend's training, but you will want to entrust your health to someone who is properly qualified.

Kinesiologists specialize in overall health care, the holistic Mental, Physical, Chemical and Energetic ("MCPE") approach of balancing the whole person. They use expert muscle testing to determine if any of the foods you eat regularly are affecting your performance and your fitness in any regard. They check you out physically and balance any structural imbalances they may find. They can also help you very simply with stress, anxieties and phobias in the mental sphere, without getting "heavy", or taking many sessions. Even if you feel fine at the moment, remember,

PREVENTION IS BETTER THAN CURE!!

It is well worth the investment in time and money spent in fees to have yourself checked out. You may find things out from your kinesiologist that will set you on the path to long-term health benefits. So consult an expert.

So to summarize:

- Safeguard your health while you have it. When it is gone it is too late.
- Eat for health by avoiding manufactured foods and preparing your own from fresh food.
- Back away from stress. Reduce the levels of stress in your life systematically.
- Get moderate exercise, and practice deep breathing. Buy and use a rebounder, and you will appreciate the amazing difference it can make.
- If you do not feel well, take action immediately.

Next we are going to cover the first part of our suggestions for better communications, and the subject is learning to listen more effectively.

CHAPTER SIX

LISTENING WITH POWER AND ATTENTION

One of the most important factors in communication and human relations is to be a good listener. People tend to like and appreciate a person who listens attentively. They prefer it when someone listen interactively, and not passively. That means making appropriate comments that indicate that you really are understanding and caring about what they are saying.

The person who consciously and deliberately listens most, usually has more power in the interchange. Listening carefully and skillfully can lead to more information being revealed than otherwise. So you learn more by listening. A lot more than you do when you are doing all the talking! On meeting someone for the first time, your listening well, can also be a big factor as to whether the person likes you or not.

AVOID BEING IN CONTROL, AND BE A LEADER.
We are going to deal with the need to avoid the use of controlling words. Everyone uses them without even realizing it. Everyone says, "You should..." or You ought to..." "You must..." Not realizing that they are being critical and controlling of the other person. We will deal with this in much more detail in the next section.

There is a trap awaiting all whose job involves advising other people. The client pays a fee to hear the expert advice of the lawyer, accountant or practitioner. Surely it is all right for them to tell their client where they are going wrong? No, that is not always what the client actually wants, believe it or not! It is far better to give people options regarding how they might consider a different course of action.

To tell others what to do, is to take control away from them. We suggest replacing that almost universal approach with the concept of offering several suggestions for the person's consideration. Then let them choose.

> **Choice is our greatest power.**
> **To take away a person's choices diminishes them.**
> **It reduces their freedom to run their**
> **own life the way they want.**

So we do not want to control the other person. If we have fallen into the habit of doing so, maybe we need to look at ourselves. Perhaps it might be a good idea to question our reasons and motives for wanting to direct and control others.

Attempts to control others invariably brings results we do not want in our own lives. It can often set another person on a wrong course, especially if we do not know all their circumstances. Or by attempting to control the direction another person takes, we may encounter resistance or hostility. Antagonizing someone is not a good course of action. Once offended, most individuals are very hard to win back.

What we do want to do however is to keep any discussion on track. This often means that it is necessary to exercise some degree of leadership over the way the conversation goes. This is a very fine line. If you over-lead, you will stifle the flow of thoughts, and if you fail to keep the matter on track, it can waste a lot of time. We will deal with the fact that most people speak to each other in a controlling mode in the next section.

AGREE WHEREVER POSSIBLE OR AGREE TO DISAGREE

Entrepreneurs are quite forceful and opinionated people. So it is a challenge for them to realize that points of view other than their own might not only exist but also have some validity.

> **Showing respect for the other person's views**
> **is part of being diplomatic in business,**
> **and in our personal lives too.**

After all, others have a right to think differently from the way we do. So it behoves us to find ways to accept, or at least learn to live with an alternative approach.

So it is wise to do your best to be an advocate, and avoid at all costs being an adversary. If your friend, relation or customer says something that you do not altogether agree with, it eases the flow of the conversation if we can find a way to say something agreeable. It is most unwise flatly to contradict anyone, tell them they are wrong, or that you do not agree.

There are many ways one might smooth the pathway to an agreement to differ. Here are a few responses we might use. They all start with the word, "Yes..."

YES, that might be one way to view it, and... YES, some people may take that view, and... YES, it seems that is the way you see it, and... YES, I can appreciate how you feel, and...

YES, I understand that is how you see it, and... YES, I hear what you are saying, and...

YES, you have made your point clear, and...

YES, you have obviously put a lot of thought into it, and

Note, these statements do not start with, "Yes but. "Which is a form of rebuttal of everything they have just said. So when using this approach and any phrases similar to those above, you are enabled to put your opinion to your friend by saying:...

- and, I have previously taken the view that...
- and, in my experience, other factors have been important as well.
- and, would you be willing to look at my proposals?
- and, does that close the door on my suggestions?

There are of course unlimited variations on this theme. It is application of the principle that is important. Sometimes if you do not wish to offer counter thoughts and suggestions, it might be possible to use words and phrases that do not commit you to agreement, yet they do show you are participating in the conversation. If someone expresses a view that you do not share, you might say, "Really.", "Oh!", "Mmmmmm" or make some other non-committal type of rejoinder.

AVOID JUDGMENTAL OR CRITICAL STATEMENTS.
One of the fundamentals of love is to allow others to be who they are, and to make make their own way in life without our negative input. Who are we to judge what others decide to do with their lives? Not only do we not have all the facts, we do not have the right to criticize others. Even when asked for constructive criticism, watch out! They may not have want hear it anyway!!

It is surprising the number of people who make incisive, provocative or critical personal comments. Sometimes even when they hardly know the person. Comments such as, "You've put on weight!", or "Where on earth did you get that jacket, a charity shop?", or "What's all this then?" as they pat your stomach. Regrettably they are displaying their gross lack of manners when anyone makes such comments.

An ancient proverb suggests that if we cannot say something nice about a person it is better not to say anything at all!

It is a positive challenge actively to think of something nice to start each new conversation. This is a very worthwhile thing to practice. It is also best to avoid telling anyone what they think or feel, and especially unwise to say that what they are feeling or thinking is wrong. If you want to know what anyone is thinking or feeling, how about asking them? It is unwise in the extreme to tell anyone what they "should" or "should not" do in their lives.

THE FIRST INTERACTION
When you first meet someone, take the opportunity to learn their name. Notice I said learn. How many times has someone said to you with abashed embarrassment, "I am so sorry, I didn't catch

your name. You are...?" On the other hand, how many times have you realized that you have already forgotten someone's name when they told you only seconds ago? O.K. Perhaps you don't, but I'm sorry to say I occasionally do, even though I know how very important it is.

If when an individual approaches you, and they say, "Are you Brian Butler?" I might say, "Yes, how did you get to hear about me? After they explain, I have some information from them which will enable me to start a conversation about things that interest them.

If a person does not immediately introduce themselves by name as you meet them, then the initiative is up to you. Rather than ask someone, "What is your name?" A preferable opening gambit is to say, "My name is Brian, (or Brian Butler if that is more appropriate), ...and you are...(pause)? They will soon fill the gap left by your question.

Because names are so important, I set remembering names as a goal. As a result I am getting better and better at remembering people's names. I had to make a special effort, but only partly because I cannot stand the embarrassment of forgetting, mostly because I really want to remember each person's name I meet. It is very important to me in my business, (and yours!) That we latch on to and remember the person's name.

One way to remember names is to repeat them back in some form. For instance, "My name is Jean." You reply, "Right, Jean, what would you like me to know about your needs?" or if you want to break the ice some more, you can say, "How do spell that, is it with an E or not?" Then they give you the name again. This does not apply if the person says their name is Susan or John! Many people have names that are abbreviations, so that gives you an opportunity to say, "OK Mike, is that short for Michael?"

INITIAL STAGES OF COMMUNICATION

This is a good time to start as you mean to go on. Adopt a listening approach, and encourage them to talk to you. Draw them out abo ut themselves and their needs and wants by interjecting questions or comments occasionally. Let them reveal themselves as much as possible. Use every snippet they give you that you think might lead to your understanding them or their needs better, by saying, "Tell me more about that."

Or you can simply say, "And. ?" That 'and' followed by a slight pause, really works wonders with someone who is quite brief, or who uses few words.

THE POWER OF SILENCE

Before you answer a question or respond to a statement - PAUSE 3- 5 SECONDS. This is a very powerful way to interact with someone. As they appear to come to the end of a thought, make sure that you allow a pause before replying. This does a number of things.

1. Pausing helps the person feel that you are giving a moments thought to what they are saying and considering it carefully rather than giving them a knee-jerk reaction.
2. Pausing avoids the sin of speaking over the next thing they were going to say. If we jump in as soon as we "think" they have finished their line of thought, and they have not, then as soon as they start their next sentence, we are already speaking.
3. Pausing helps avoid an even worse sin. If we kick in too soon, we prevent them from completing their thought, and expressing themselves fully. This may cause them to feel frustrated, or even to forget what it was they wanted to say next.
4. If we come back too fast, it can also imply that we have not really been listening whole mindedly to them, but have been thinking about what we are going to say next while they were talking. An amazing proportion of people do this most of the time. It is a particularly distressing habit of "Type A" people who are go-getter achievers.

So, while you are listening, LISTEN. Thoughts of possible responses may come to you as they speak, and concentrate on listening!

When they appear to have come to a pause, wait 2, 3, 4, or 5 seconds before you say anything. The time lag will depend on how it feels. If the pause is too long, it will appear artificial, and that is the last thing you want. Pause just long enough for you to gather your thoughts and decide what to say next.

LISTEN 70% - TALK 25% - PAUSE 5%

In any conversation, attempt to listen at least 70% of the time. This means we speak for less than a third of the time. This may not hold true when you are asked to explain something to a client. Then you may need to reverse the percentage, but it is still an excellent plan to keep the client in the "discussion".

This may be done by checking regularly with such phrases as, "What is your reaction to?" or "How does that feel to you?" or "What type of further information do you need on that topic, before I move on to something else?" "In which way do you think this applies to you?"

Of course if both parties know this aspect of good conversation, you will have a battle on your hands for the one who listens most! I heard about the twins that were finally born after being in the womb for years. Apparently they were both such gentlemen, that every time an opportunity came to be born, one would say to the other, "After you." And the other would say, "No! After you!"

USE OPEN QUESTIONS THAT START WITH HOW, WHO, WHAT, WHERE, & WHEN

Make your "open" questions start with Who, What, Where, When, How, then you will be sure to get some more information, and you will have prompted your prospect to think more about the subject. Notice one of these interrogatives is missing, the word WHY. This is because without realizing it, this can put people on the spot, or maybe they will feel "on the spot" and have to justify what they think. This we do not want to happen.

As you listen you will form a picture of what it is this person wants from you, wants to achieve today, this week, and maybe long term. Let them tell you about themselves. This, apart from hearing your own name, (so address them by name from time to time as you ask a question) is what people most like to hear. After all, what is going on in their lives is the most important thing to them. And so it should be.

AVOID CLOSED QUESTIONS

Closed questions start with verbs. Do you...? Have you...? Is that clear? Will you. ? These are called "closed" questions, because the person can simply say, "Yes" or "No" and the line goes dead for a moment or three. Then you are on the spot to think of another question if they make no comment.

WHAT TO DO IF THE CONVERSATION DIES

If the person "dries up", use phrases like:

- Tell me more about..................
- For example?
- And...?
- When you say that, do you mean..?
- What about your (job, spouse, kids, house, journey, etc.)

INTERRUPTING - DON'T

Avoid interrupting. Listen. Only interject if you need clarification. Then use the "active listening" responses:
- When you say,... what do you mean?
- Could you expand on that please?
- In what sense? Etc., etc.

We will be covering "active listening" in more detail later.

NO-NO RESPONSES

It is not best to use the frequently used form of question, "Do you understand that?" or "Is that clear?" These are "closed" questions used by many presenters. The answer to that type of questions is almost ALWAYS "Yes". This is because the person does not wish to appear "thick", or "dim".

YES-YES RESPONSES

Sometimes you want a client to say, "Yes". So, phrase your question carefully about something you are quite sure they will say "Yes" to. In this case it might be a good idea to use closed questions so you are more likely to get a one word response, either, "Yes", or "No"

WATCH OUT FOR SEMANTICS

Origin: Gr. semantikos, significant from semainein, to signify.
Definition: Pertaining to meaning in language. Subtleties of meaning, often used derogatorily.

What do you think might be the reason that people respond negatively to someone being specific and exact about the words they are using to convey a particular sense or meaning?

What might provoke someone to say, "you're only using semantics. "Well, it could be that they do not want to deal with the reality of the meaning of the words, but only their illusion as to what they have allowed themselves to think they mean.

For example:
What do you think the word 'sophisticated' means? How about, well-bred, well-educated, knowing how to behave well in public, exercising good taste, up-market, suave, poised, etc.?

Would you accept some of those, or what would you say it means?

The dictionary says of 'sophisticated', one having acquired worldly refinement, urbane, cultured, elaborate, suitable for or appealing to the tastes of sophisticated people.

The same dictionary says of 'sophisticate' is to cause to become less natural or simple, to be more worldly wise, to make less true, genuine or honest, corrupt pervert, or adulterate.

The root of sophisticated comes from the Middle English sophime, from the Old French sophisme, from Latin sophisma, from Greek sophizesthai, acquired skill, clever device, to play subtle tricks.

We have the word 'sophistry' a plausible but misleading or fallacious argument. So it sounds good, but it is false. 'Sophist' Any of a class of ancient Greek philosophers active during the second half of the 5th century B.C. who specialised in providing instruction in ethics and the art of public speaking. And came to be disparaged for their oversubtle self-serving reasoning and devious argumentation. Now I wonder if that has anything to do with philosophy! Philosophers are looked up to as respected thinkers, who form the bases of educated thought. Aren't they?

Definition: Philosophy, Love and pursuit of wisdom by intellectual means, the investigation of causes and laws underlying reality. Inquiry of things based on logical reasoning. The system of values by which one lives.
Definition: Philosopher, A student or specialist in philosophy. A person who remains rational and calm even under the most trying of circumstances.
Origin: Gr. Philosophos, "loving wisdom" philo-love sophos-wisdom!

But did we not read the meaning of sophos under sophistry as clever, skilled in specious argument, false reasoning, trickery.

Even the dictionary falls into defining a word according to its popular usage, choosing to ignore the negative aspects of the root upon which it is based.

It pays to be cautious about the words we use, and how we interpret what others say to us when we are listening to them. If ever in doubt as to the meaning of what someone is saying, it is always wise to ask them. You can always say something like, "I'm not sure I understand exactly what you mean." Or you might say, "I'm not sure I understand exactly what you mean by " Whatever the word or phrase they used that you were not sure of.

MANNERS MAKETH MAN

It is a real pity that manners are declining in our society. Good mannerly behaviour is a sign of culture, education, and consideration for others.

Each of us can be a committee of one, to make sure that we pay attention to our own manners.

Hopefully seeking to improve them. It pays to be careful not to be influenced negatively by those around us, who may not have had the advantage of much training in good manners.

If you are a good listener, it will build your rapport with others. They will tell others what a good conversationalist you are. They will say what a sympathetic person you are. As a practitioner, one of the most important tools to keep sharp, is your listening skill. You will be well on your way to making another "Ambassador" who will provide an annuity for you for years to come. People feel much happier if they are sure that you have not only listened to them politely, but that you have heard what they said, and that you really do understand what they mean by what they have said.

LISTENING AND CARING BUILDS TRUST

Doing business with anyone anything comes down to trust. Do they trust and like you? Will that trust last beyond this conversation or this sale? As we befriend our clients, we go beyond the straight commercial interchange. We give the client something of ourselves to take away with them. In their turn they leave something of themselves as we develop friendships in our business relationships.

You never know for sure that a customer is sold until you have their money in full. Sometimes we have clients who have insufficient money with them to complete the purchase of all the items they need and want. The principle here is to get the "goods" into the hand of the customer as soon as they indicate they want them. Assuring yourself that they will be paid for is, of course, vital.

We do not accept credit cards, and the person may not have a cheque book with them. So what we do is, to look them in the eye and say, "That's OK, you were probably expecting it to be less.

Please take the goods with you, and send us a cheque, or pay us for them next time you have an appointment with us.

We do the same when people proffer a cheque card. Our response to being offered guarantee cards is, "We do not need that thank you, we trust our clients, and they never let us down." This reinforces the feeling of trust that is developing between us.

We also sell courses that cost thousands. When that sort of money is involved, if clients are not paying in full up front, careful agreements need to be clear between the parties. If people want to take advantage of time payments or monthly installments, we have to explain that it will cost a little more to cover interest and charges at the outset. All that is part of the deal. All part of the process of arriving at a win-win situation for both the customer and ourselves.

It is important to treat everyone with great respect especially where money is concerned. Just because someone is a bit hard up at the moment, that is no reason to look down on them. Most of us have had lean times at some time during our lives, haven't we? Almost everyone has been broke at one time or another.

If we can find a way to help a person finance their purchases from us, we will always bend over backwards to find a way to help them if we can. This way we have made some more friends. Oh, occasionally, very rarely in fact, we might be let down by someone, but I emphasise, it is extremely rare. Quite a few people we have helped in this way have turned out to be our most loyal supporters. They especially appreciate the fact that we helped them out when they really needed it.

KEEPING IN TOUCH - SHOWING THAT YOU HAVE "HEARD" THEIR NEED

Depending on the way your particular business works, it is a good idea to send out letters or emails to all your clients periodically. This is especially important if someone has not been back to you for a while.

We all need encouraging reminders. Have you ever had a recurring thought, "I must make an appointment with so-and-so", but it keeps slipping your mind? Have you ever kept putting it off for no really good reason? Most of us have done that from time to time.

So send a nice letter out. No pressure, just a friendly letter, letting them know that you are thinking about them. Everyone likes to get letters like that from people they like - and they like you because you took the trouble to understand that, should be back in six months, diarise a date five months hence and write them a letter or an email.

If they are worded correctly, warm and friendly, and contains no pressure, chances are they will appreciate the reminder. They will be much more likely to call for an appointment, or visit your business than they would without the tactful gentle reminder. This will increase your business.

A telephone call is often very well received, provided there is no pressure. Work out a script of the sort of thing you want to say. List the main points you would like to cover if you get to speak to them and not an answering machine.

If your client is a man, it is often a good idea to call during the day. Yes he will be at work! But with luck, you will get his wife, or another member of the family. Ask them to make a note that you called.

Then when your client comes home from work, someone hopefully will say to him, "Oh! By the way so-and-so called, and asked after you. They said there was no message, and only to call them back if you thought you would like to."

It's quite nice to get a message like that. The fact that someone was thinking about you is always nice to know, so long as they do not think the only reason you called was to get more business, rather than to give them something if it is only you best wishes.

If you do get the answering machine, you will want a very brief script to help you leave a short and to the point message. You might want to say you were thinking about them. You may want to give a reason, like you were going through your records and came across their client record card, and that prompted you to call. You may want to add that you hope all is well with them and their family. Or, whatever else might be appropriate to your particular business. It will pay to give some thought to this idea, and what you will want to say to keep it short and sweet.

You do not even have to ask them to call you back. In fact, it is sometimes powerful to say, "You don't need to call me back, unless you would like to."

Appreciating the power of listening in establishing good communications can lead us to success faster. It is not necessary to control people to be successful, in fact the opposite is true.

You cannot motivate people, because they can only motivate themselves. We can however inspire them to greater effort. Being agreeable wherever possible, avoiding being judgmental or critical and being a leader not a controller is the way of the successful person.

Our first interaction with people creates an impression that cannot be easily undone. There is an enormous power in silence and just listening 70% AND SPEAKING 30%. When we use open questions starting with how, what, where, etc, we invite the speaker to let us have more information.

It is bad manners to interrupt. It is good to elicit "Yes" responses whenever possible. When we handle our conversations with tact and diplomacy, and listen interactively, we build mutual trust. Keeping in touch helps us to build our network of friends, and it costs so little in time or money.

So in summary and review, here are headings we covered in this section: Listen with power and attention, by taking an intelligent interest, and helping to lead but not control the conversation.

Agree wherever possible, or agree to disagree. That it is best to avoid judgmental or critical comments, especially personal ones. How to make the first meeting with someone work well. Remember that a person's name is one of the most important sounds to them.

We talked about the power of silence and pause, and that our aim is to listen about 70% of the time. Closed questions that start with a verb will be answered by a yes or no, open questions that start with who, what, where, when, how, usually encourage more information.

Semantics can lead to misunderstandings, but manners maketh man.

Listening politely builds trust, and keeping in touch with people shows we have at least partly understood their needs.

In the next section, we are going to go carefully into the matter of control, and the words used universally to control others.

≈ SUCCESS ≈

CHAPTER SEVEN

THE SCOURGE OF THE 4-LETTER WORD

PROCEED WITH CAUTION

I feel that I should begin this section with a somewhat sober warning. Because of the nature of the content of this section, we strongly recommend you do not show this book to others, or play the tapes to them in an attempt to enlighten them.

The person or friend you most want to share this with may not be seeking enlightenment. In fact, they may resent your attempts to share it with them. They may even get very angry that you are learning about things they do not want to look at in their own lives. Jesus said,

**Cast not your pearls (of wisdom) before swine,
(people who are not yet ready to treasure them),
lest they turn and rend you. (Rip you apart verbally.)**

I hope you will not feel the need to try it. But if you do, it will not be long before you really upset someone. So learn from my mistakes. I've done it, and ruined relationships.

So if anyone is not interested, it is vital that this is respected. As we will cover later, one way we show love to others is to respect their wishes. That includes minding our own business, and not making any attempt to change other people's behaviour to suit ourselves. Or worse still, trying to help them in a well-meaning way. If ever you feel tempted to do that, trigger this thought, "Mind your own business!" **"MYOB!"** Then imagine this inscription on your gravestone: "This person meant well!" You bought this programme for you, not for others. You have it because you are open to making changes in your life. You were willing to pay the price in hard earned cash to get your hands on it.

It is important to recognise that others are not necessarily interested in personal development, so do not push it.

Much of the material in this programme, if implemented with enthusiasm, will cause you to make considerable changes in your life. People will notice. If they express interest, give them the fliers, and tell them you can get them a copy and that the price is so-and-so. That will probably be enough to put them off! Unless that is, that they realize the real value of the material. The worth of these hundreds or thousands of keys to success is measured in millions not tens, or hundreds.

One way changing your attitudes and behaviour can affect you, is you may find that you no longer want to spend quite so much time with certain people. It may be you will not feel like continuing to pursue some types of activity that are not helping you to make positive progress in your life.

Often when people you have previously spent a lot of time with realize that your direction has changed more than somewhat, they may be hurt or offended. When some people get hurt, they lash out at the person they think is causing them the pain. Others may just walk out of your life. Remember,

"Birds of a feather flock together."

So when you were as you were, you spent time with those who held similar views about life as yourself. As your perspective of how you want to conduct your life changes, then so will your feelings towards different people. It also may affect the way they feel about you.

This particular section contains some pretty strong stuff. It will confront, and highlight common destructive behaviors that everyone uses. It will show that many of the mechanisms we spend a lot of our time using in our communication with others, just doesn't really work for us or them beneficially. Hence this rather sober beginning to this section. We certainly want you to get the maximum benefit its contents. What we do not want, is for you to precipitate reactions from others, by sharing information with them that they may not be ready to receive yet.

IMPROVING OUR INTER-PERSONAL COMMUNICATION

We may sometimes wonder why we do not get what we want. We cannot understand why we get so much of what we do not want! I trust that this section may shed some light onto that problem, and help you begin to solve it and get more of what you **do** want.

As you are successful in so doing, you will start to change the way you speak to others, and the outcome will be much happier both for you and for them. Then you will discover that you are attracting less of what you do not want into your life and conversely you are attracting a lot more of what you do want.

The way most of the world's population communicates does not always seem to work very well. Marriage and relationship breakdown is at an all time high. Marriage counselors invariably put this down, at least in part, to a breakdown in communication between the couple. Listen to mothers in the supermarkets as they attempt, often with little success, to control their small children.

Children's conversations when they are at play are a prime example that the desire to control others starts at a very early age. One child is usually telling the others what to do. "Now you do this, and I'll do that." or "You're supposed to..." or "Everyone put their dolls down and come over here." Then perhaps, "If you don't do this, I won't play with you!" An early example of emotional blackmail! Or "I'll tell your mother!" An example of threatening and controlling behaviour.

Harmless enough, you might say? Far from it!

These children are forming the manner they will use to deal with the world when they are adults. It can be hilarious, and saddening to watch, and listen in to their chatter, (unobserved of course) and analyse which of the controlling words and emotional levers they are using on their peers.

It is not only children who indulge in this type of interaction. One way to make a study of the worst examples of this type of conversation among adults is to watch television "soaps". These contain endless examples of unbridled attempts to control everyone else's life, while making a complete mess of their own.

These soap operas on TV are thick, sickly slices of rich town, poor country, or any other variety of the human condition. They are presented to the unsuspecting, hapless viewer who thinks they are harmless fun. They are not. They are "brain-messing", (the opposite of "brain-washing!) propaganda that makes for misery and negativity. They are a waste of your valuable time, and we have discussed the value of that!

Soaps offer "escape", but escape to what? To an unhealthy diet of "soap cake".

Sickly sugary emotional topping, fruity nutty characters, and floury folk who often do not know what day it is. Just listen to a soap with a paper and pencil handy, and write down every instance of the use of the twelve destructive communication categories listed below.

Watch, and listen to how they criticise and control each other. Look how they indulge the lowest of human tendencies, in their greed, avarice, lust, infidelity, gossip, backbiting, mis-judging, criticizing, undermining, rejecting, attacking, hating, complaining, the list is nauseating and endless. If that is supposed to be an escape, I would rather stay in the "prison" of normal life!!

The directors and writers of these shows know exactly how to titillate the audience, and keep their tens of millions of viewers on the edge of their seats. They know just how to get people to talk about the plot and the characters on the way to work, or in the office, and set them up to wait with impatience for the next episode to find out what happened. People actually write in complaining about the actions of the actors and actresses, as if they had actually been doing in real life what they were portraying on the screen!!!!

By the bye. Apparently some psychologists have decided that children's behaviour just might be affected by what they see on the TV screen. This has been hotly refuted by "experts" for decades. A child can spend more hours in front of a TV before going to school, than they will spend hours in front of a teacher during their whole school life. And some thought that would not teach the kids anything or influence them????????

So we watch how people mess up their own lives, and then adopt the position of teacher to tell others how not to! This is the extraordinary thing. We spend most of our lives bumbling around not exactly building and maintaining perfect relationships, making a fair few mistakes in the way we run our lives, and then spend the rest of our time telling others how they should or shouldn't live theirs! Oh dear!

RECOGNIZING THE DESIRE TO CONTROL
Anyone who wants to control, may need to look for someone who is willing to be controlled, unless they want a fight on their hands. So, on the other hand, we can reflect on the way those who are being "organized" or controlled, respond to the attempts of the bossy boots to control them. "I don't want to play with you you're bossy." Which reveals the resentment at being told what to do. or "I don't care if you do tell my mum, I'll tell her that you. " which establishes a "tit-for-tat" routine which certainly persists into adult life.

Guess where these dear little children learn these attitudes and manipulative ways of dealing with others? Why, from their parents and other adults, of course!

Controlling, or attempting to control is part of the basic fabric of our standard social behaviour.

Most adults are not nearly as happy as they would like to be in life. Part of the reason for our lack of joy may be the devaluation and denial of our almost our every expressed thought or action by what others say to us. And it often seems difficult to pin down exactly why a happy joyful life eludes us. That is why we have devoted a whole section to seeking, finding, sharing, and enjoying happiness in this programme.

It is certainly possible to fall into a pattern of using these same controlling techniques, in a desperate attempt to maintain what little control over our lives we can. We do not always realize that this very activity is counter productive, and we finish up alienating people by criticizing and controlling them against their will. We have already covered the concept of "Self-Talk" where we criticise ourselves, thus reducing our self-esteem and feelings of self-worth. When we feel bad about ourselves, the immediate tendency of the carnal mind, the raw unbridled human nature, is to lash out and criticise others. We seem to think that if we can make someone else feel badly about themselves, we will feel better in our misery. Nothing could be further from the truth.

TWELVE COMMON TYPES OF COMMUNICATION THAT DO NOT WORK WELL

In many of these instances, there is a right use of the concept. If someone is about to step out in front of a bus, then "ordering" and "warning" are certainly very much in order.

In each case here, the problem is with the person who is initiating the controlling approach. The person speaking is assuming a role of superior judgement. From the position of the person commenting, the other person's feelings, attitude, decisions etc., are either not valid, or relatively invalid. Being invalidated is an uncomfortable and destructive experience.

1. **Ordering, Commanding, Directing**
   Give him a piece of your mind. Tell him to take a running jump.
2. **Warning, Threatening**
   If you don't.... I warn you.... You'll be sorry if.....
3. **Moralizing, Preaching, Should, Ought**
   I don't think that's the right thing to do. You should... You ought to know better.
4. **Advising, Offering Solutions, Suggestions**
   Why don't you.... What if you... You should... You ought to... You must...

5. **Teaching, Lecturing, Logical Argument**
   If you look at it this way..... It's perfectly clear that.... **Surely** you can see that if this is that, then these are those!
6. **Judging, Criticizing, Blaming**
   It's wrong of you to.... I think you are going the wrong way about it... She was wrong to do It's all your fault anyway!
7. **Sterotyping, Namecalling**
   What a rat! You're stupid!
8. **Interpreting, Diagnosing, Analyzing**
   Maybe you could.... If you had said..... Surely you could... What you need to look at here is....
9. **Patronising**
   For someone with your talents, that's quite good.
10. **Accurate evaluation.**
    What you have just said is going to rebound on you because you are trying to control someone else's life.
    (This may be a perfectly accurate observation, but unless they asked for your evaluation, do not be tempted to give it. And even if they did ask, be careful, they may not really want it!)
11. **Questioning, Probing, Interrogating**
    What happened next? Why did you do that? Why?
12. **Withdrawing, Distracting, Diverting, Humouring**
    Maybe it's not so bad. You may be imagining things. It's all in your mind. Oh, if you think so, you may be right.

A couple of approaches to be careful with. It is not wrong to praise, or to be supportive, of course not. It is not good to be patronizing or overly sympathetic

Praising, Agreeing.
I think you were really smart ... definitely! That's just the way it seems to me too.

RELINQUISHING THE DESIRE TO CONTROL

We want to give you some absolutely priceless keys. Keys that will unlock the secret to better communication. Changing the way we use a few little words, will unlock the doors of a verbal prison, and set us free to enjoy a new way to communicate.

Most people are completely unconscious and unaware that the way they speak to others frequently conveys covert or blatant attempts to control or direct their minds, or their activities.

A large part of everyday conversation consists of people in various subtle ways of controlling, or attempting to control others.

In order to change our mode of communication it is necessary to understand the words and the syntax that are used in the controlling process.

When people use the phrase "four-letter words", they are usually referring to curse or swear words. The type of language which is generally considered unacceptable in polite society. (Although the media is gradually changing this by permitting foul language to pervade the television programmes. It is also now common in films designed for adult viewing, which often end up being watched by young children who are not being properly supervised!)

We are going to borrow the phrase "Four letter words" to describe graphically the no-no words that are in common everyday usage by virtually everyone. Why are they no-no words? Because they are the words which are used in an attempt to control, direct, or call into question the other person. They can infiltrate practically every sentence of a "normal" conversation.

So how is our communication frustrated? All our lives, we have been called into question, and required to explain ourselves in response to abrupt demands. Even worse, the person to whom we are speaking, does not allow us to express or to feel what we really NEED to express or feel, because they use various forms of rebuttal or disagreement every time we say something.

This type of communication is highly destructive, drives people apart, and exacerbates friction and disagreement. It also prevents business people from achieving the best either for themselves or for their clients.

By the way, the use of these words is so deeply ingrained in our minds and our lives, that it will probably take some time of focused effort to begin seriously to eliminate them to any degree. After twenty-five (now fifty-five!) years of practice, I still trip up from time to time.

THE FOUR LETTER WORDS

Here are some typical blocking forms of rejoinder which use "four-letter" type words:

"Yes, BUT". Some folk use this as a start to any response to anything you might have said. "Yes, but..." Actually means, "No! You are wrong, or You have left something out that is vital, or, the bottom line: "I do not agree with you at all!"

BUT is the great negator. If I say, "You look great, I love your hair, that get-up really suits you, but..." The person to whom you are speaking is now waiting for the knife to go in, they tense themselves for what you are going to say next, because they know it is going to be bad!

The only valid time to use BUT as a negator is to dispel and soften the impact of some bad news. For instance: "You forgot the butter, and you didn't mow the lawn yesterday and now it's raining, BUT I love you for being you." What the BUT does here is to reduce the significance of the criticism. You may forget this or that, BUT you are great! Have a go at using it in this positive way, instead of the other negative manner. You will probably enjoy the experience.

Probably the most frequently used "four-letter" word in the English language is **YOU!**

You? Yes! **YOU!**

If **"YOU** is followed by any insistent, verb, instruction, evaluation, criticism, or negative statement it is classed as a "four-letter" word and is a blatant attempt to control or direct another.

Examples are:

"You **should**...", "You **shouldn't**...", "You **ought to**...", "You **ought not to**...", "**You must**...",

"You **must not**..., "**You can't**...", "**You idiot!**", "**You're wrong!**", "**You must be joking!**"**, the list is virtually endless.

Watch out for your usage of the word, **"YOU"**, it will change your life!

TRY to... is a phrase interpreted by the brain as confusion. If I say to you, "Try to pick up that pencil.' You will probably pick it up. But if I say, "I did not say pick it up, I said, 'Try to pick it up.'" You will then experience some mental chatter and uncertainty. Try implies an attempt. An attempt does not necessarily include success. When we tell children to, "Try again.", to "Keep trying.", without realizing it, we are sometimes perpetuating their inability to actually do it.

Nobody ever "Tried to climb Everest", or "Tried to win at Wimbledon." They say instead, "I'm going to conquer Everest." "I am going to be champion this year at Wimbledon." Do not be tempted to say that this is just semantics. Words have incredible power.

"Try" is a weak and ineffective word. Being told to "try" results in a weaker and less effective attempt than being given, or giving ourselves the instruction to "Go for it with all our might and main!" or just "Do it!"

"Why?..." (The dreaded "WHY?") From earliest childhood, we have been asked, "WHY?" Why did you do that? Why didn't you do that? Questions of this nature call us into question. They put us on the defensive. It is an emotionally charged word which usually stirs our emotions negatively.

When we are asked, "Why?" We are being required to justify ourselves or explain our motives. We are being questioned, and asked to explain our reasons for doing, or not doing something, but the very question, "Why..." has the implication that the questioner does not approve at some level. In my work, I often need to know why someone chose to do something in a certain way. So I choose to start my enquiry with, "What prompted you to do it." or "What was behind your decision to.." "How did you decide on that course of action?" or in some other way ask the question but by all means avoid the word "WHY". It is longer, but better. You may want to experiment with this yourself.

"**SURELY** you don't mean...?" "**SURELY** you ought to..."

Surely in this context might roughly be translated, "Surely, you wouldn't say that!" (Implying only a half-wit, a moron, or an ignoramus would!) It is a real word of condescension, of looking down on anothers feeble attempt to do something their way.

"**I ASSUME...** Let us break it up. "I ASS-U-ME that you mean..." To **ASSUME makes an ASS out of U and ME!** When we assume, we do not really know at all. We are guessing at what the person means. We can be wildly wrong, especially since most people do not say what they mean anyway.

This could be for several reasons. First, they may not have thought through thoroughly what they really want to say. Second, they may not really know what they mean at all. Third, they may just have blurted out something without thinking first. This will become clear when we get into the next section on deciphering the "code" that is used by practically everyone most of the time.

A preferred response if we are not clear what someone means might be to say something like. "I'm not clear what you mean when you say..." They will then rephrase it, and maybe it will become clearer.

ALWAYS AND NEVER. There is no such thing as always and never! The usual vernacular is, "You ALWAYS do that..." or "You NEVER do that..." Neither statement is true. It is a false accusation. It is an exaggeration. It is an unfair criticism.

It is best to avoid using ALWAYS and NEVER in reference to people's behaviour. The sun ALWAYS sets, and the moon

NEVER shines, it only reflects light, but even there, the use of always and never might be all right, and it is good to avoid using them without careful thought.

CAUTION - USE THIS INFORMATION CAREFULLY

The use of these "four-letter" words and these types of response are habitual for most people. It is the norm. When challenged about it, most people will usually say, "I didn't mean to . . ." and will attempt vigorously to justify their well-intentioned replies.

Your friends and relatives may even accuse you of being "too sensitive" or of "taking things too personally", or "using semantics" when you object to some of the sentiments expressed by using the rejoinders above. You may now realize that in reality they are direct insults, which can be very hurtful and cruel.

> **All these "four letter" modes of response tend to invalidate the feelings and the statements that the person is doing their best to convey to you.**

This lowers their self-esteem, and makes them feel that their opinions, feelings and decisions are not worth anything. This in turn enables them to feel misunderstood, and unaccepted.

It is strange that we might be quite inept at managing our own affairs, but when it comes to other's problems, the solutions seem so obvious to us, we wonder how it is that they can be so blind as not to see them!!

So someone might say, "Why did you do that? Surely it was obvious? I can only assume you didn't know. You always put your foot in it! You never seem to think first! You really should try not to jump to conclusions like that! You may mean well, but look at the result!"

That previous paragraph contains most of the commonly used "four- letter" words. I am certain, however, that it sounded like a perfectly normal comment. That is just the trouble. Comments like that are so common that they are accepted as the norm. That does not reduce the often unrealized pain they cause.

**We have a wonderful opportunity
and a great responsibility when we are
dealing with another person's feelings.**

When someone entrusts us with their inner sensitivities, their fears, hopes, dreams, ideas for the future, it is our privilege to treat that trust with great respect. Respect is the first pre-requisite basis for a truly loving relationship. As we work to eradicate the use of "four letter words" from our everyday life, we will become much more aware of the disparaging nature of most conversation. We will notice more and more that the average discussion involves a lot of cut and thrust.

A shocking example of people in high places indulging in rudeness, belittling, contradicting, and in the verbal put-down, is the way politicians talk at each other in the British Houses of Parliament.

We have discussed the "soaps" which display in the main so-called "working classes" gently, and not so gently, destroying each other with their words.

So from the "high" to the "low" in our society, the thread that runs through most communication is a form of battle. The weapons of attack, control and counter-attack are the "four letter words".

Most find it a long hard battle to get to grips with changing the habit of a lifetime, as they notice their own tendency to include "four letter words" as they speak.

Adopting this new form of conversation, avoiding the tendency to control, judge and criticise, takes vigilance, and thought. It also takes a strong intention and determination to make the change.

Others may well notice that you are taking a different approach from the way you used to talk. They may like it, they may ridicule you, they may want to know what the difference is, because they will probably not be able quite to make it out. They will know that something has changed, but they may not be able to put their finger on it.

But take heart, it is a very worthwhile struggle. The rewards are greater peace, kindness, gentleness, and love in our business dealings, and also in our private lives.

So in summary: Be careful not to share your enthusiasm for the information in this programme you are learning with others around you, it may offend.

This section is about ways to improve our communication with those we love and care about, and those we work with.

What qualifies me to write about this? The fact that I have made so many mistakes over the years by not applying what I knew. This especially applies to techniques of communication and money making concepts. I can tell you where I went wrong in the hope that it will save you a lot of grief.

Once we recognise our inherent desire to control, or to attempt to control others, we are on the way to solving it. So we looked at twelve ways people use words in an attempt to control you, your actions, or your feelings.

When we really realize our controlling patterns, we can relinquish them, and use gentler and kinder words which accept more in a right spirit of meekness and consideration for our fellow human beings.

We started with a caution, and we end with one. Be very careful please, not to use this understanding to "technique" anyone, or God forbid, to get one over on them. This understanding is to be used in humble service to one another to smooth the pathways of good straightforward conversation.

Changing the way we think, and express ourselves is a lifetime's work. We will never get it completely right, but is rewarding in the process of doing our best to get there.

Next we will look at how to draw them people in conversation, and find out what they mean, and how to own our feelings and how to encourage others to express theirs.

CHAPTER EIGHT

PEOPLE TALK IN "CODE"

Most people talk in "code". How are you?", We ask. "Fine", they reply. What does "fine" mean? Are they better than yesterday? Are they feeling energetic? Are they worn out and fed up, but just saying fine because they do not want to burden you with their problems? Who knows! Unless we recognise that "fine" is a code word, and delve a little deeper, we will never know.

So when we listen carefully to people, and we hear statements that are non-specific, non- explicit, or all embracing, our communication with others will improve dramatically if we "DECODE THE CODE"

To use our communication skills effectively in assisting people resolve their problems and achieve their dreams, one needs to be a good listener. It is necessary to be constantly alert for the little clues which will lead enable us to understand them better.

One of the secrets of being a good friend is to LISTEN carefully which subject we covered in a previous section. Sometimes the most innocent comment someone may make, may yield enormous mileage in helping our understanding of them, so it pays to listen to every word for its true meaning.

Clarity of communication is rendered further more difficult by the use of codes.

I may be very frustrated, and when someone asks me what is wrong, I may say "I'm fed up!", or "I'm cross" or I may even reply, "Nothing!" Remember everyone's greatest affliction is lack of self-esteem, even when you think the opposite, so look for ways to help people build theirs. It is a key to your happiness and theirs.

Once upon a time, I was talking to a friend and she said, "I'm having a 'bit of a do' in the garden on Saturday afternoon, would you like to come?" I said, "I'd love to."

I turned up at about three p.m., for her "do" in the garden, wearing my old gardening boots, an old jumper full of holes and jeans which were faded, torn and frayed with my trusty spade over my shoulder. As soon as I walked in to her house, I knew I had failed to check the "code".

GOING "UNDER THE CODE" AND LISTENING TO DECODE THE "CODE"

The house and garden were full of people dressed quite formally holding glasses of champagne in their hands. It was actually a farewell party for the Chairman of her father's company on his retirement?

When I was invited to the "do", this was "code" and did not convey to me the real nature of the occasion at all. I should have said, "When you say would I like to come to a "do", what is involved?" My friend would have replied, "It is the farewell garden party for the Chairman." I would have known immediately what I should do.

> **People speak CONSTANTLY in code. People rarely say what they REALLY FEEL AND MEAN.**

So when you realize that your conversational partner is saying anything that is not being clearly expressed, or you are not absolutely clear about, go "under the code".

For instance if a friend says, "I'm fine thanks." You might reply," When you say you're "fine" today, its great to hear that, and I had heard that you were going through some heavy duty problem or other. Then they might say, "Yes, I was, and it still is hanging over me, and I am quite concerned about the outcome, but I'm feeling fine in myself."

This technique is extremely useful in any counselling situation where an individual needs to be heard and to get a problem out into the open. Utilizing "under the code" enables the helper to facilitate the person really getting into their feelings. This makes for much more effective balancing since they are firmly "in the mode"

REMEMBER - LISTEN FOR ANNOUNCEMENTS
On the other hand, if you listen carefully enough and long enough, people invariably say what they feel in their inner selves in one form or another. Listen for subtle, or not so subtle "announcements". Sometimes just one word is sufficient to let you understand how a person is really feeling.

For instance, you are conversing with someone about holidays. You are talking about your holiday in Greece, the coach ride from the airport, the lovely hot sun, the delicious food, and the beautiful views. During the conversation, your friend might say, "I hate those long transfer times."

You can just continue with your chat, but make a mental note of that strongly worded emotional statement. "I hate..." is a strong word, expressing a strong sentiment. It is also an "announcement."

If you catch the announcement, then you can immediately go "under the code" and help them to express their true feelings if that is appropriate. It is unusual to be "heard". Most people do not listen to each other, much less respond to the true nature of the feelings each is expressing. Human relationships blossom when communication improves.

So when you have finished telling you friend about your holiday, and it is time to move on to a different topic, you might say, "You mentioned you hate long transfer times, did you have a bad experience?" Then your friend will regale you with the way they really feel about a disastrous holiday which started with a four hour transfer time from the airport, including a choppy crossing to a Greek island when they were violently sick. You may not have really wanted to hear all that, but your friend will have noted subliminally that you were really hearing and caring about what they said to you.

PEOPLE REVEAL THEMSELVES AND THEIR FEELINGS BY WHAT THEY SAY

There is untold value in this brief Biblical quote from the latter part of Matthew:12:34 ... **and out of the abundance of the heart, the mouth speaks...**

Those words are worth burning into your brain. People will reveal the innermost feelings of their hearts, often without their realizing it. All we have to do is catch the sentiment by listening carefully. If you are not sure exactly what it is they are saying, then is a good time to go "under the code".

Be very cautious when discussing anyone's feelings. One thing to avoid at all costs, is to tell someone else how they are feeling. That is like handing them a hand grenade with the pin pulled out. Wait five seconds only for the explosion! It is usually all right to ask, "Were you angry about that?" But, remember the danger of the word, "YOU". It will blow up in your face if you say, "You were angry!"

People often say things, and when challenged on it they may say, "I didn't mean it.", "I don't want you to think that...", or "I was only joking" etc., Remember that the thought had to be conceived in their heart or mind to be expressed. There was some truth in what they said they just do not want to admit it!

GO UNDER THE CODE, BUT DO NOT PRY

Be careful not to use going under the code to pry into someone else's feelings where they would rather you did not go. This going "under the code" is a very powerful tool to be used in real love, and not ever to manipulate or coerce anyone to reveal more about themselves than they wish to.

You can always check if it is all right to proceed. Simply ask, "Is it all right to talk about this?" Watch carefully for another coded response! They may say "Certainly" and mean the opposite. How many times has someone said, go on tell me where I'm wrong, I want to know... and then gets upset when they hear the worst! If someone says "I'd really rather not talk about it, that is our cue to show respect and not pursue that matter until we are sure the person wants to. It is unfortunately true, that once words have been spoken, we cannot unsay them. Here is a treasured quote from a famous poem.

> **As an arrow loosed from the bow,
> so a word once spoken cannot be recalled.**

and on the other hand,

> **A word fitly spoken, is like apples
> of gold in pictures of silver.**

Words have such force, such power! It really does pay to use them thoughtfully and carefully. Some say choose your words carefully, They couldn't be more right.

THE POWER OF FEEL-WANT-WILLING

Those three words strung together like that may not mean too much, but they represent one of the most powerful communication tools I know. The proper use of this formula helps me and others to "decode" coded statements, and facilitate both myself and others to express true feelings.

Most people only talk about what they 'think', not feel. If you want to talk about a "problem" with the hope of clarifying the situation, or with the possibility of finding a solution, one way to handle it is to use "Feel-Want-Willing". For instance, I can use it to express my needs, and let the other person know how I feel.

CAUTION: This is another potentially dangerous situation. That word **"YOU"** is lurking, but never to be used in going "under the code" unless it is included in a question. I hope this will become clearer in a moment.

1. Explore for yourself how you really do feel about the issue. Define the issue in your own mind. Think it through carefully if you have the opportunity to do so. At least pause for thought before attempting to deal with the subject.
2. State clearly how you **FEEL**, define it carefully in the first person.
3. State what you **WANT** to see or achieve as a result, or results.
4. State what you are **WILLING** to do towards the end you desire.

If there is no positive response to Feel -Want-Willing, it may not be a good idea to pursue the point with this person. It is often better to leave a topic to another day, or not attempt to deal with it at all rather than risk causing a rift between yourself and the other person. If it is absolutely impossible to talk about the topic, and work towards resolving the feelings, the you might be forced to another realization. Another conclusion may be that there was no relationship existing in the first place.

If you do want to use the word **"YOU"** in order to find out about how the other person feels about the situation, as already stated, form the FEEL-WANT-WILLING formula into questions. So so you might ask questions of another:-

- What do you feel about that?
- What do you want?
- What are you willing to do?

**It takes guts to risk saying how we really feel.
We draw back in fear of offending
or spoiling the relationship.**

If the other will not cooperate, after a few attempts, you may have to conclude that no proper relationship exists between you anyway, so you really cannot lose.

A lot of people are in 'relationships', both sexual and non-sexual that are in truth not really 'relationships' at all in the true sense of the word. To have a relationship with someone, one basis has to be the ability to communicate and resolve matters of importance between you by patient, kind, loving discussion.

INTRODUCING A NEUTRAL THIRD PARTY

If you have a real problem with someone, one way to handle it is to ask someone who knows you both, to ask you how you "feel" what you "want" and what you are "willing" to do. Then the person acting as a neutral third party peacemaker can go to the other person involved, and ask them the same things then mediate between you until the "steam" goes out of the situation.

You can also do this, by telling a mutual friend what you FEEL, WANT and are WILLING to do in respect of some current situation. This may work well, and it might blow up in your face if your mutual friend misinterprets, or misrepresents your statements. There is really no substitute for going to a person face to face to discuss any problem or any issue if that is at all possible.

ACTIVE LISTENING - A POWERFUL COMMUNICATIONS TOOL

When we talked about listening in a previous section, we discussed the merits of passive and active listening. "Active listening" is a wonderful tool which can be extremely useful in helping someone define their real feelings.

We use active listening when the other person has a problem - be it difficulties at work, an unhappy relationship, or any kind of negative feelings - e.g. inadequacy, frustration, rejection. It is imperative to have permission to use active listening, so always check, "Are you happy to talk about this?" In other words whenever the person begins to express feelings, we can use "active listening" to assist the person to open up and explore the root of their problem. This is especially effective for occasions when the person is talking in "codes" and is unclear as to exactly what they are feeling.

When we are communicating in this way, we have a responsibility to be completely accepting and non-judgmental of that person.

It is imperative that we genuinely want to take the time to help them to find their own solution to their problems. It is vitally important also that we do not allow our own feelings about the situation to enter into the dialogue. The purpose of this exercise is to provide an opportunity for them to take time to unburden and clarify their feelings, without any additional input from us.

There are various errors that people can make when using "active listening" - above all, this is not a tool with which to "technique" people. It should only be used when we have been specifically invited to help. It is possible to manipulate the person into feeling a certain way using active listening and this is a gross violation of that person's trust in their relative, friend or colleague. It is also a tragic mis-use of a wonderful tool that should only be used in loving service to others.

Extracting intimate feelings and information from someone and to use it against them is exceedingly destructive. If we do not have enough time to hear the person out, it is best not to even begin to "active listen" with someone - since it will only lead to their feeling unfinished or frustrated. When using the type of responses that are effective in "active listening" it is crucial that we feed back our understanding of their emotions with empathy, and do not just parrot their words back at them. If we simply repeat the emotion words they have used, this will only serve to irritate them and distress them.

For instance, if someone says, "I hated him when he said that." And you respond, "You hated him." They will say, "That's what I said!!" A much better response might be, "You felt furious?" Then the person with the problem will either use your new word, or contradict it. For instance, "You bet I was furious, I was beside myself." Or they might say, "I wasn't really furious, more just a feeling of deep dislike." So the person has been able further to define their own feelings about the situation.

A good listener will keep up with whatever messages the subject is currently expressing - not lag behind or return to a previous paragraph in their monologue. That would merely serve to "drag up" stuff that has already been dealt with in a way.

**Active listening is not a tool to use to probe
Deeply into someone or to overemphasize
The intensity of the feelings heard in the process.**

Sometimes it is clear that the person needs another form of help other than "active listening", in which case it is respectful if we back off, and give them their space to act in whatever way is most helpful to them.

Maybe they need to talk to the person concerned. Perhaps they need to take decisive action. They may have realized in just starting the conversation that they do not need to talk about it any more, but resolve it by doing something.

"Active listening" involves listening carefully to the subject with an awareness of their needs. Listening to analyze the words they use to find the expression of their true feelings. The job of the skilled "Active listener" is to "hear" and help the person who is attempting to express their feelings, clearly to "define" them. The "Active listener" can help by reflecting back to the subject, a brief paraphrase summary of the feelings they heard.

The subject will then clarify whether the listener has understood clearly what they were feeling. If the subject does not feel the "Active listener" has understood, they will respond with different "feeling" words which more closely explain their emotions.

Feelings are "feelings". Interpreting these sensations into words is difficult, and sometimes virtually impossible. Our thought forms feelings and pictures inside our brains, and our hearts, are much richer than any language, or anyone's vocabulary can adequately express.

When through being actively heard someone is enabled to express themselves freely and expansively, without interruption, denial, contradiction, disagreement, judgments, ridicule, or any other form of rebuttal, the sense of relief is often profound.

It may be the very first time in their lives they have really, truly felt "heard", "understood" and "accepted". A wonderful feeling for them to experience, and for the listener to share!

Useful Active Listening Responses.

All these responses are framed as questions, NOT as statements.

- "You feel (felt, will feel, may have felt etc)… ??????? (followed by any verb of emotion, "hated", "loathed", "detested," etc., you thought they wanted to express)
- "You wanted. ?(followed by a summary of what you think they want)
- "You mean?. ?(followed by what you think they DO mean.)
- "And… ? (when you feel they have more to express on the subject.)
- "Like…?(a [noun], a person, an experience etc) "You see (saw, will see etc) it as. ?"
- "Really?… "In what way?…"In what sense?…
- "The reason being?… Because?…
- "As in?… "Similar to   ?
- "From what point of view?… "Concerning?…
- "You remember it as…? "It seemed. ?
- "You'd rather?…"You heard it as…
- "Relating to…? "It appeared to be…?
- "You think…? (thought) "Instead of…?

These possible replies are just suggestions. When using "Active Listening", it is essential to be natural, and say only what feels right. Use all the tact that you have at your command.

WHEN SHOULD ACTIVE LISTENING BE USED

There are very clear ground rules about when this approach is appropriate. Here are some of them:

1. When the other person OWNS the problem feels any of these, rejection, angry, overloaded with work, inadequate, or any other negative emotion about any person or any situation.

WHY SHOULD THE PERSON SOLVE HIS OWN PROBLEM

1. They have more of the data than anyone else.
2. They are the one to implement the solution
3. It builds their own self-confidence
4. It helps them to be responsible
5. It keeps you in the role of facilitator

UNDER WHAT CONDITIONS SHOULD ACTIVE LISTENING BE USED

1. When you hear feelings, whether confused or clearly expressed.
2. When the person says he has a problem
3. When the person sends messages that are not easy to decode
4. When you feel genuinely accepting
5. When you really sincerely want to help
6. When you want to and are able to take the time
7. When you have TRUST that he can find his own solution
8. When your own feelings are not involved in his problem

This last point is absolutely crucial. Active Listening should never ever be used when you have a problem with the person, unless you are sure that you will be able to keep your own feelings from coloring the discussion.

WHAT ARE THE COMMON ERRORS WHEN USING "ACTIVE LISTENING"?

1. Using "Active Listening" when the person is a problem to you
2. Using "Active Listening" to manipulate the person into feeling the way you think that they "should" feel.
3. Using "Active Listening" to get information after which you move in and use the information to hurt them.
4. Using hit and run "Active Listening" - not staying to hear him out.
5. Feeding back their emotions with no empathy
6. Lagging behind - two messages back
7. Going too deep - interpreting what they say
8. Undervaluing or overvaluing the intensity of feelings heard
9. Parroting the feeling words vs using "Active Listening" synonyms of the meaning of the feelings
10. Using "Active Listening" when the person obviously needs some other kind of help
11. Active Listening when you have not been asked or invited to help

WHAT ATTITUDE SHOULD YOU HAVE WHEN YOU ACTIVE LISTEN

1. They have a right to feel the way they do
2. I respect you as a person
3. I really want to hear your point of view
4. I am not judging you.
5. I do not necessarily agree or disagree
5. Your feelings belong to you
6. I trust you to handle your feelings - to solve your own problems

WHAT HAPPENS TO THE OTHER PERSON WHEN YOU ACTIVE LISTEN CORRECTLY

1. Makes the other person feel you are not trying to change them
2. Encourages the other person to continue communicating - to say more, to share their feelings
3. Encourages the person to go deeper
4. Facilitates self direction, self responsibility and independence
5. Helps the other person to release feelings and free themselves of their negative control over him
6. Promotes a relationship of warmth and closeness
7. Facilitates problem-solving in the other person - produces insights, new understandings
8. Encourages the other person to be more open to your rejoinder reflected thoughts and ideas
9. Helps the other person shift focus from "outside self" to "inner self"

The use of "UNDER THE CODE", the avoidance of "FOUR LETTER WORDS" and the careful, loving employment of sincere "ACTIVE LISTENING" produces a vastly different feeling between two people than usual methods of talking about life's problems.

Solutions would become apparent, different approaches would present themselves, events are seen in better proportion, and peace and harmony would be preserved.

Now we are going to look at the difference between Knowledge, Understanding, and Wisdom. This material hopefully will help you utilise the information in this programme in the most effective way.

KNOWLEDGE - UNDERSTANDING - WISDOM

We live in an information age. Knowledge is increasing at a rate which would have been unimagined just a decade or two ago.

What is this "new" knowledge all about? Is it bringing happiness to the human race. Is "Surfing the Web" going to be the "New Jerusalem", or could the web and the net be a trap for the unwary?

Few would disagree that we live in a world which could do with more love, understanding, kindness, patience, and other virtues which were at times in our history, part of our educational programme. Sadly, little if any of these and other spiritual qualities find their way into the "National Curriculum".

KNOWLEDGE

Knowledge consists of facts, figures, and details about the world about us. Someone might know for instance that electricity comes into their house and makes the lights work. They might be able to turn the television on, and be able to adjust the thermostat to make the room warmer. They may have more knowledge about wiring and fuses and circuit breakers, and when to push one in if the fuse blows. None of this knowledge needs Understanding.

We seem to have little knowledge of the type of communications between people and nations that will bring about an uplifting result. That is why we included a section in this programme/

UNDERSTANDING

Understanding involves knowing HOW things work, and how things happen in our complex world. Understanding the way electricity is made, how Ohm's Law helps us understand the relationship between volts, current, resistance, and wattage power.

Understanding about the intricacies of Electricity is a background to the Knowledge we have about the appliances in the home which enrich our lives. The more understanding we have about our world, the more enriched we are. It helps us make sense of the senseless and apparently illogical things, the mysterious happenings which are part of everyday life.

None of this Understanding is necessary to make things work for us, but Understanding leads to an opportunity to use those things over which we have control and dominion thoughtfully.

How much understanding is there about our modes of communication. People are still arguing whether violence on TV affects children. And whether there is any value and benefit from taking Vitamin C!

WISDOM

Using things thoughtfully does not necessarily mean that Wisdom is involved. The Human race is supposed to be evolving. Some think we are getting more and more wise, and more and more spiritual, and that we are improving as time goes on. (?)

Certainly we have more knowledge, and a great deal more understanding in every area of life, and is it producing a more beneficial result?? This needs careful, objective, non-emotional consideration.

The exercise of Wisdom involves using the Knowledge, and the Understanding in such a way as to bring about a result or outcomes that benefits all. Wise use of information and understanding should help us to avoid disastrous mis-uses of knowledge and understanding.

The story goes that there were two little green men in a space ship. They happened across the Milky Way galaxy and decided to have a look around. They swooshed from here to there, and were struck by the incredible beauty of the planet Earth, so descended to have a closer look.

Using superior technology, they were able to determine that we were an advanced society, and had many things they understood. Then reading some very special equipment, they observed nuclear reactors, and even saw an experimental nuclear explosion take place in the middle of the sea.

Immediately, they set course away from the Earth at top speed. One little green man said to the other, "We know a lot more than they do about nuclear science, that is evident. I cannot believe my eyes, they are tinkering with nuclear fuels, fission and power on their own planet!!!"

This is not a "ban the bomb" statement, merely a story to illustrate a point.

Some say a little knowledge is dangerous, in some cases a little knowledge, say of mouth to mouth resuscitation could be a life- saver. All generalizations are incorrect - including this one!

CONCLUSION

All the knowledge in the world, all the understanding in the universe, with as much as you can get of both, without Wisdom, we are lost. With all your abilities, strive for wisdom, and once attained, hold on to it.

So in this section we have covered how people talk in "code", and how we can decipher that without prying, listen for important "announcements'. Deal with sensitive emotional issues with "FEEL, WANT, WILLING".

How to use "Active Listening" to help people explore and deal with their own feelings, and how Knowledge, Understanding and Wisdom in our communications can help us get on better with everyone.

In the next two sections we will cover the important topic of money.

CHAPTER NINE

MONEY, PROSPERITY AND WEALTH

MONEY MAKES THE WORLD GO ROUND

Many people think that there is something "not quite nice" about money. Some feel jealous of people who have money. Others think money is somewhat vulgar! "Money can't bring you happiness.", Some say triumphantly, feeling rather smug in their self-righteous poverty.

Some mis-quote the Bible, (as so many do!) saying, "Money is the root of all evil." What it actually says is that "the **LOVE** of money is **A** root of ALL evil.." Clearly money is not the root of ALL evil. Lust is the root of some evil, so is jealously, or envy, or hate and none of these is necessarily connected to money. Another statement in the Bible says, "My friends, "..I wish above all things that you PROSPER, and be in health..".

**The truth of the matter is that money
makes the world go around.
If we did not have trade, then we would
not be able to buy the goods and services we need.**

Many feel we must be careful not to focus on money, or the things it can buy. They think that in the vigorous pursuit of it, there is a danger of moral turpitude. No doubt, if you pursue affluence to the exclusion of, or at the expense of other important values, you may "gain the whole world and lose your soul."

MAKE FINANCIAL INDEPENDENCE ONE OF YOUR GOALS
- **However, it is wise to make financial independence One of your primary goals.**

There are several reasons for becoming prosperous:

First: Once you are not wasting energy fretting and worrying about how you are going to pay your bills and survive reasonably well, you can devote more time to other more important values in your life.

Secondly: If you make financial independence one of your major goals, in order to be financially independent, you will have to develop the kind of character you need to become. This is a major key to success.

We need to set goals which will cause us to become the person it takes to achieve them. Reaching the goal of having lots of money is the secondary aim. The primary aim lies in the person you have to become to reach it. It is not the money or the millions that are most important, it is what you must do and become, in order to be a millionaire. This is a vital concept to understand.

Many so-called "lucky" ones win the pools or the lottery. Virtually everyone who becomes a millionaire in this way is broke within a few years, because they had never developed the strength of character it takes to manage wealth. If you win a million, you had better think and act like a "millionaire" quickly, or you will lose the lot!

Thirdly: You can only help others, like your immediate family, and maybe close friends if you yourself are in a strong position financially.

Fourthly: Learn to live on 70% of your net income. Allocating the thirty percent: First 10% saving for prosperity. Second 10% for capital you manage. Buy something and fix it and sell it. Indulge in capitalism and commerce. Bring goods and service to the marketplace. Third 10%, a fund for charitable causes. Be careful with charities, as they usually eat up to 90% in expenses so your money does not get to where you want it to go.

Fifthly: Live within your means. The reason most people reach retirement age with little savings or resources is because they lived beyond their means for so many years. A little bank loan here, (paying interest and getting nothing) a few items purchased on the credit card there, (paying extortionate interest), another car they could not afford, a holiday they so badly needed but did not have the money for, etc. etc.

* Living within your means is a good habit, just like living beyond your means is a bad habit.

If you have that tendency, think about making some changes. Downsize your ideas and wants to fit what you can afford. "Cut your suit according to your cloth!"

If you have too little money, find a way to make some more cash in the spare time you would have if you watched less television, or spent less time at the pub, or on the golf course. If you want more money for your needs or your wants, it is out there for you. It just takes work and discipline.

THE ALLURE OF "EASY MONEY".

Some folk waste a lot of time in their lives dreaming of easy money. Of course a few win the lottery or the pools by the sheer chance of 14,000,000-1 odds. Some few may make money on Penny Shares or Futures Options, but it is not those who have failed to study carefully, and know nothing about the markets. It is a real trap to spend your time and your life dreaming of "easy money".

There are more people who want to sell you a get rich quick scheme than you can shake a stick at. Hundreds of "Business Opportunities" are offered in glowing and seductive terms. Once you reply to one, you will receive several plans a week from those who have bought your name and address from a broker. Most only want a few pounds, or a hundred or two, and they'll tell you how to make your fortune. Perhaps their scheme might, but proceed with great caution.

Think very carefully before you involve yourself with multi-level marketing or telephone selling. Particularly, do not buy a large stock of any product unless you have experience of how well it sells. There is no such thing as "easy money".

BECOMING A MILLIONAIRE, OR AT LEAST WELL-OFF - BY SAVING!

There is a wonderful little book called, "The Richest Man in Babylon". I wish I had read it when I was sixteen, and then every year ever since. It tells how to become financially independent as you go into your middle age. * The secret is simple. All you have to do is to save a proportion of your money, and never spend it.

What you do with what you have, is so much more important than how much you have. Most people save up for something special, and then splurge all they saved, and more. They never leave the money in the account to grow. Even worse they probably put the rest of their lust bill "on the plastic". Start saving! If you don't do anything else we suggest in this programme, however old you are, and whatever your financial position, **start saving.** The majority reach retirement age with little or no savings. Many companies give concessionary rates to "senior citizens" on the assumption that they will be poor. Do not let yourself get to your later years poor! Start saving **NOW!**

Here is the difference between a "poor" attitude, and a "rich" attitude beautifully put:

> **Poor people spend their money on what they need and save the rest. Rich people save some money and spend the rest on what they need.**

How much should you save? It seems that 10% works best. Ten percent of the money you have to use after the government has taken its bite might seem a lot, and it is. By the way, don't begrudge paying tax, it supports the country and the system that enables us to make a living in relative peace and safety.

But here is the magic. After a very short while, you do not miss 10%. You actually don't. You were hard up before, always finding it a battle to keep up with the bills. That does not change immediately, but you don't really miss the 10%. Somehow, it doesn't make bill paying any more difficult.

It is quite incredible that once you make the commitment to put a small amount of money away regularly that you never touch for any reason, your finances will start to pick up. They will. There is an eternal law at work. Just do it and see for yourself. If you start saving a little early enough, at age twenty or thirty, putting money away you never touch, you will retire rich.

Say you keep saving just £10 a month, and put it in an envelope, or under the mattress. After a year you have £120. At the end of the second year you have £240, then 360, 480, 600, 720, and after seven years you have £840. Not bad sum, but no interest!

An employee had been given a certain amount of money to take care of for seven years. To be on the safe side, our careful friend buried it. When the rich man came back and asked for his money, the chap dug it up and gave it back to him. The rich man exclaimed, "You could at least have put it into a building society account, and I would have had some interest, you're fired!"

The magic ingredient to savings plans is Compound Interest.

So what is saving just £10 monthly worth with compound interest? Compare how it grows when 10% interest is added each year? At the end of the first year you have £132. At the end of the second year have £277, then £436, £612, £805, £1018, £1252.

So in seven years with compound interest, your £840 invested has gained 50% of its value and become £1252, and you did not have to do a thing. Now you have over a thousand pounds behind you would never have had if you had not put away a measly ten pounds a month.

Now if you had put away a hundred a month! After only seven years you would now have £12,520. That is how it snowballs - fast! Since originally writing this book interest offered and paid on savings had steadily decreased, so that now, you are lucky to get 1% or even less!)

You want to be a millionaire? About £200 a month for thirty-five years will accrue to a million or more if invested at 10%. This can be achieved with careful selection of savings scheme.

After twenty or thirty years, the growth due to compound interest becomes phenomenal. But it only works if you do not spend it. So what is the money for? When you no longer want to work so hard, say when you are fifty or sixty, you can afford to take it easier, knowing you have a million in savings! You can live very well on the interest!!

"Oh! But I am too old now!" Some might say. Although the benefits of saving are much greater when you start young, it is never too late to start operating this vital fiscal principle. Check out several savings schemes with a responsible certified financial advisor.

Once you have signed up, don't leave making payments to chance. Fill in a standing order form, and send or take it into your bank. Then forget it, apart from doing your accounts monthly. Just let it tick away until you realize you are a bit better off than you were, and then raise it!

When you watch a goodly sum grow in an account which you do not touch, it gives one an entirely different view of money, For one thing, you're never broke. You may not have much money to spend in your pocket, but you're not without funds. And that is a very good feeling.

AVOID "INSTANT GRATIFICATION"
* If you are tempted to raid the larder and buy a new stereo, or a new car, avoid the temptation to give in to "Instant Gratification." Remember to put "Delayed Gratification" into gear instead. Take a grip. Be disciplined now, you will be more than glad later, when you are a millionaire. And you can be, really!

SPEND NOW - PAY LATER, THE SEDUCTIVE FLIERS CRY
At times, in certain economic conditions, you can't get a loan for love or money. Other times, with the economy in a slow period,

lending institutions are falling over themselves to let you have as much on loan as you will take. "You can have 20,000 to buy that car, or that boat you have always dreamed of.."

Suckers fall for this appeal to the human nature desire for "Instant Gratification". Don't wait until you can afford it, your kind finance house will lend you the money at only base rate plus 4%. What they do not tell you is that the boat or the car will cost you almost double by the time you have finished paying for it.

WATCH THOSE CREDIT CARDS!

During periods when money is plentiful, (and it should be since they are continually printing more which devalues it!) obtaining money on a credit card is child's play. This is another subtle way of getting you to pay extortionate rates of interest for indulging your desire for "Instant Gratification". After all, we are told, it is only one and a quarter percent interest each month, and you get six weeks free credit until you have to pay for it.

Most credit card companies charge interest from the moment you make the purchase if you do not pay off the entire amount within the time allowed. It is true that you can have several weeks free credit, but only if you pay the whole amount within the time allowed.

Be aware of another slight misconception here. Your payment takes several days to reach the credit company. So even if you think that you have paid it off in time, you may well have missed the due day because of a weekend, a bank holiday, or whatever which delayed your payment reaching the credit card company. Then you will charged with the interest on your next statement.

O.K. Here is the rule, an absolute rule of life. It is a law of fiscal wisdom:

Never, ever use a credit card to buy anything you want that you cannot pay off the full amount well before the due date.

Let us put it another way. You might get three percent if you leave your money in a building society for a whole year. The credit card company will take three percent away from you in a few weeks. One and a half percent a month is about twenty-four percent a year.

If you cannot exercise the self-discipline, never to use your plastic cards for "Instant Gratification", or for things you want rather than things you really need, and only then if you can afford what you need, CUT THEM UP, and THROW THEM AWAY. It is a pity to do this, as they are a great convenience.

So use your plastic card as a convenience only. First calculate your average monthly expenditure on incidentals you purchase regularly, and make sure that you set that aside in an account to pay for them as if you were paying cash. Then buy your fuel for the car, and other running costs with your card. As soon as the credit card bill drops through your letter box, pay it. Do not delay. Do not do it tomorrow. Pay it NOW!

HERE IS THE OPPOSITE OF SPEND NOW - PAY LATER

One key to saving money is called "Delayed Gratification". What exactly is "Delayed Gratification"? Well it means the opposite of "Instant Gratification". So that when you get the urge to buy something, or spend some money, you stop, wait, and think: Do I really need this now, or can it wait a while? Can I really afford it?

You might think you can, so here comes the killer question. "Can I afford it, AND keep to my savings plan?" If the answer to that is "NO!", put "Delayed Gratification" into gear.

Remember the adage: People buy what they need, but they spend money on what they want!

Buy what you think you really need NOW, but keep your savings plan going. This is paramount. If you do keep "raiding the larder", when you go there one day, it will be bare. So grit your teeth and put "Delayed Gratification" into gear. You will never, ever be sorry you did.

BE YOUR OWN LOAN SHARK!

Suppose you cannot talk yourself into "Delayed Gratification" on one particular occasion. Then it is perfectly legitimate to go ahead and indulge yourself occasionally. There is only one proviso. If you take any money out of your "Prosperity Account" it must be put back, plus interest. Plus interest? Yes!

Find out how much a finance company would charge you monthly for so many months, to purchase the item on terms. Buy the item out of your own funds, and then pay that additional amount into your own "Prosperity Account" until it is paid off. That way you will be in profit with yourself!!

BUYING YOUR HOME

When it comes to mortgages, the lending policy of major institutions has certainly changed over the years. When I was in my twenties, working for one of the largest building societies, the investors received interest at the rate of 3.5%, and the borrowers paid 5.25% on their mortgages. This was a differential of 1.75%, which was used by the society to cover operating costs.

Incidentally, not a lot of people know this, but building societies were established and run as non-profit-making concerns. Interesting that most of them have now turned themselves into banks or bank type operations which do make a profit.

Have you noticed how banks will generously give you 2.5%, or 3.5% when you leave your money on deposit. But when you take out a mortgage they charge 8% or 8.5%, or even more! That is quite a huge differential of around 5.5%! This gives rise to huge profits over the usual period of the loan which is about twenty-five years.

There are a couple of powerful ways to save money when you buy a house. Firstly, buy one that is less than you can afford. Have you ever noticed that the price of the house you absolutely must have is just 10,000 more than you can really afford, but that is the one you want.

You want this particular house so badly, (you want "Instant Gratification, NOW") that you ask to have your mate's part time pay taken into account so that you can get a bigger mortgage. You stretch yourself to the limit, and ask for a thirty year term instead of twenty-five years, because the monthly payments are a little lower, not realizing what a difference it is going to make to the final cost of your house.

So let us take for an instance, you buy a house for 110,000, and you put 10,000 down as a deposit, and take a mortgage of 100,000. Here are the exact figures quoted by a mortgage company at the moment of writing this.

100,000 over 30 years, @ 7.15% monthly repayment is 675
30 x 12 = 360 monthly payments of 675 = 243,000

So to borrow 100,000 for thirty years, you finish up paying nearly a quarter of a million for your home! And for the privilege of reducing your monthly outgoings by about 41 pounds, (or dollars) you finish up paying an extra 28,200 for your home over the thirty years compared with a twenty- five year term.

Here are the figures for a twenty-five year term:

100,000 over 25 years, @ 7.15% monthly repayment is 716
25 x 12 = 300 monthly payments of 716 = 214,800

Now look how much your house costs you if you reduce the term even more, to twenty or even fifteen years.

100,000 over 20 years, @ 7.15% monthly repayment is 784
20 x 12 = 240 monthly payments of 784 = 188,160
100,000 over 15 years, @ 6.80% monthly repayment is 887
15 x 12 = 180 monthly payments of 887 = 159,660

Taking the mortgage over a fifteen year term, you save 83,340 compared to the thirty year term. That is almost enough to buy another house! So here is a suggestion. If you are considering buying a property, work out what you can definitely afford to pay out each month on the mortgage, not forgetting that you have rates and utilities to find as well.

Whatever the sum you decide you can afford, contact the mortgage company, and ask them how many thousand you can borrow over fifteen years, or twenty at the absolute maximum, for that monthly amount. Then add your deposit, and that is the amount you can afford to pay for your house. After a few years, with inflation, and as your income rises, you will find that the mortgage payment gets easier and easier to pay. So it might pay to stretch yourself just a little bit at the beginning, but not too much, as if you should be foreclosed upon, that can be an extremely costly business. It is far better to "cut your coat according to your cloth!" Stay within your means and rejoice each month that you are not finding your mortgage a strain. All this because you exercised a little self-discipline, and stayed with what you could afford.

Dicken's Mr. Pickwick is still right, hundreds of years later. Income £1, expenditure 99 pence, result happiness. Income £1, expenditure 101 pence, result misery. Some things do not change with time. The problem is that money on short term loan is a very expensive luxury. When I was a child, moneylenders were somewhat looked down upon. They charged high rates of interest, like 10%! This was described by the "dirty word" usury.

Shylock of Shakespeare fame, was not noted for his merciful approach when a creditor could not pay. Neither are moneylenders today. Pay up, or before you know where you are, you will have the "heavies" at your door. These people make a living by terrifying people who are poor payers. Those who get badly behind with their payments, soon get to dread the knock on the door of the collector's men.

BEWARE OF BEING A GUARANTOR

Here is a proverb about being a surety: "If you have shaken hands on a deal to be a surety for someone, you are snared with the words of your own mouth... get yourself out of it quickly!" If they do not pay, you may find the debt collectors at your door, and you are guiltless in the matter, except you signed as a guarantor. Not a wise thing to do.

IF YOU ARE EMPLOYED, MAKE YOURSELF INDISPENSABLE.
How? It is really easy! Here are seven suggestions:

1. Be punctual, not everyone is. You will be noticed if you are. Arrive early, and leave late.
2. WORK - DON'T TALK! Many people in office jobs spend far less than 100% of their time working. All too often, the first hour in the morning is spent "getting organized" and chatting about the events of last night. It is all too easy to goof off, and waste a lot of your life gassing about trivia. This in essence, is stealing from our employer. Sure, everyone needs to socialize a little, but a little is a little.
Then there is a coffee break, then after a short work break, good heavens, it's lunchtime already! And so the day flies by. Before you know where you are it is time to go home. Did you earn your money that day? When you pay someone in your own business to do work, you will appreciate how the above feels!
3. Study how to do your job better. Ask your boss what he would like you to do, in order to do a better job. Ask him for feedback on how you are doing. Very few do.
4. Think of the business as if it were your own. It will make you more conscientious, and is excellent mental practice for when you do have a business of your own.
5. Get your work done, and ask for more. Nobody does that! Maintain an industrious attitude. You are paid to work, not sit idle.

6. Dress smarter, and wear better shoes than your colleagues.
7. Learn how the business works. Watch for where it does not work. Make tactful suggestions. Determine that when you run your own business, you will be the best employer in town.

START THINKING NOW ABOUT HAVING YOUR OWN BUSINESS ONE DAY

The whole work ethic is changing. It used to be a person sought a safe steady secure job with a pension, joined a firm, stayed there for thirty or forty years, and then retired. This is almost a thing of the past. There is virtually no such thing now as job security. Downsizing is the new buzz word, but it means no job.

The number of people working from home is rising astronomically. Companies are paying staff to work at home. It is cheaper than providing staff with office space! The number of those opting to work for themselves is also spiralling upwards. You will never make a lot of money, or be in control of your finances as long as you are employed. Start working on the idea of having your own business.

Think of a good idea. Do something nobody else is doing, or do something much better, and give a better service than anyone else.

Here's a powerful concept: Start a company, build it up with one thing in mind - to sell it.

Someone I know did that, and just sold their little computer business to a major computer company for millions. You can do something like that if you put your mind to it. Look for ways you might earn extra money, but don't give up your day job! There are many traps for the unwary.

One of the richest men I have ever known gave me a piece of extremely valuable advice: "STAY WITH WHAT YOU KNOW."

Find out how better to exploit what you know. You can make a lot more money with what you already know than you realize. Apply your mind to being more effective within your own field. If you are in the wrong field, change it. Become an expert in something else. But stay with what you know! Capitalise on any personal interest you have of any subject. Whether it be fishing, (one of the biggest businesses there, is) computers, design, woodwork, kinesiology health care, or anything that can be used to bring specific values to others.

Exploit what excites you. It might be the key to your own successful business. Once you have an idea to make some extra money, pursue it. Do not be tempted to jeopardise your day job, but do get started. Do not be afraid to start small. Start with a small stock, or in a small way, but keep thinking BIG!

Think BIG, but start small!

To quote that marvellous old motivational genius, Mr. Parker:

The most important factor is to have FAITH, CONFIDENCE, and BELIEF in your PRODUCTS, SERVICES AND IDEAS.

Here are the sub-headings covered in this section on finances and business:

1. MONEY MAKES THE WORLD GO ROUND. If we did not have trade, then we would not be able to buy the goods and services we need.
2. It is wise to make financial independence one of your primary goals:
    a. You don't waste energy worrying about bills.
    b. You can spend your time more productively
    c. You develop beneficial character traits.
    d. You learn to live within your means.
    e. You work from a position of strength to help others
3. Live within your means
4. Avoid the trap of so-called "easy money".
5. Become a millionaire, or at least well-off by saving.
6. Avoid "Instant Gratification".
7. Spend now - Pay later is absolute folly.
8. Watch out for credit cards, interest is wasted money.
9. Learn "Delayed Gratification", the opposite of buy now-pay later.
10. Save money, be your own "loan shark".
11. Buying a home and taking on a mortgage.
12. Beware of being a guarantor.
13. If you are employed, make yourself indispensable.
14. Think about starting/developing your own business, however small.
15. Stay with what you know
16. Have Faith, Confidence, and Belief in your Products Services and Ideas.

The next section explores ways you can build a new business or develop an existing one.

zz SUCCESS zz

CHAPTER TEN

MORE MONEY, PROSPERITY AND WEALTH

SEED SOWING TO GROW YOUR NEW BUSINESS

Once you have a marketable product or service, put the word out about it. Tell the filling station attendant, the check-out girl in the supermarket, the milkman what you do. Tell as many people as you can about your project. Work at it in such a way that it does not interfere at all with the energy you put into your job. Be careful that your employers do not hear about it, they may see it as a threat and fire you.

Keep sowing seeds. I also run a successful training academy for those who want to learn more about being creative with their own health and well-being, or enter the complementary health field as a practitioner. If you think that might interest you, write to the address in the resources section for more information.

There it is. Simple isn't it. For all I know, you may write, become a prospect, and eventually buy more of my books or take some courses with my organization. You may not, but someone else will. You were not pressured, I simply sowed a seed in your mind to find out more if you should so desire. So tell people what you do. Don't be shy! Share what you do with everyone with whom you come into contact. Sow seeds. You will build your business.

SUCCESS IN LIFE IS A NUMBERS GAME

As a young salesman, I soon found out that the more calls I made, and the more people, I talked to the more sales I made. If you contact twice as many people every day, you influence twice as many people, you will make twice as many sales as you did before.

Selling more does not mean using high pressure methods. The very idea of pressuring another human being to do anything is to be deplored.

Remember the adage: People buy what they need, but they spend money on what they want!

BUSINESS CARDS ARE A VALUABLE TOOL - WINNERS USE THEM FREELY!

It is an excellent ploy to carry business cards and a descriptive leaflet with you wherever you go. Give them out freely. Use them to get yourself some referrals.

Give people who really love what you do a bunch of cards, and tell them to write their name on the back of each one. Then when they give them to other people, and they contact you, you can ask, "Who gave you my name?" or "How did you hear about us?" and they will know. For every one who contacts you, and gives you a name, send them a thank you, or a small gift, or a note that they have £x off their next purchase from you. If you go to public meetings, or give talks, you can hand out your cards to the audience. What about where you buy petrol, or groceries, or restaurants you eat in? Your butcher, the supermarket check-out person, the list is endless.

Do not forget the fact that you, and those to whom you relate, know a lot of people. Make sure every one of them knows what you do, and what services you provide. Don't be shy!

EXPAND YOUR CONTACTS, SELL YOURSELF TO AS MANY PEOPLE AS POSSIBLE

Most people when they start out in selling, sell to their friends and relatives first. This way they get a start, but often those folk only buy from them because they want to help, or they feel sorry for them. It is not a good idea to rely on friends to buy.

Build a prospect list as you go through life. Everyone you meet, if there is an opportunity to tell them a LITTLE, a very little, about what you do, do it. If they show even a tiny bit of interest, say, "Thank you for your interest, I'll send you some information through mail if you like. May I make a note of your name and address? Ask, "Do you know anyone else who might benefit from what I do?" Also include that question in any mailings.

Build up your own name and address list in this way. Each one could mean a lot to you. A list built up in this way is worth far more by thousands to one, than one purchased from a list broker. It is your list. You built it from people you know.

STORING NAMES AND ADDRESSES AND SENDING EMAILS, PRINTING LETTERS & MAIL LABELS

If you haven't yet got a computer, do get one. Even if you can't afford it. These days you cannot afford not to. They will save you an enormous amount of time if you control it and do not get carried away.

Do not be dazzled by all the talk of Windows this and that, or that you have to have sixteen megabytes and a two gig hard drive. Yes if you are going to use it full blown for your business, but you won't anyway if you cannot afford it.

When I was first in computers, our rented machine from IBM cost £2000 per month to hire. It had 2k. Yes, 2K!! We did a huge volume of work on it much, much faster than doing it by hand.

Computer hardware is going out of vogue within eighteen months now. That means that you can buy something that is three or four year's old for a song. Remember, that three year old machine was the bees knees when new. When it first came out it was the fastest thing on the market. Now people look down their noses at it because it is old. Old it may be, but it will do a great job for you. A darn sight quicker than keeping a card file, writing or typing individual letters, or addressing envelopes by hand.

You can now buy a modest 486 with 4 or 8Mb memory and a 540 megabyte hard disc and a small floppy drive for about £200 - £250. A second hand dot matrix printer for about fifty, or a good secondhand laser printer for a £100, and you are in business.

By the time you read or listen to this, these figures may be way out of date, and even humorous to see. One thing is absolutely true, is that it always pays to buy good used equipment, well behind the current cutting edge of the market, if it will do the job for you. That principle will never change. Starting out with shiny new of everything has brought many a person starting out to their knees because of the bank loans it took to finance those grandiose ideas.

A simple word processor, and a simple merge programme for address labels, and sending emails and your power to spread the word is powerfully enhanced. Buy one today.

If in doubt about exactly what to get, talk to someone who has done it first, preferably not a salesperson. If they start talking about Pentiums, and Giga this and that, tell them you want to start small and inexpensive. If they continue to bluster about gigabytes and old things being useless, end the conversation. Find someone who will talk about it in terms that you understand and can afford.

Incidentally, for your interest. I have a Ford Scorpio, top of the range, air conditioning, electric windows and sun roof, heated seats, you name it. It has even got electric heated wing mirrors! It is nearly ten years old now, but it had been well maintained from new. It cost me £1700 five years ago, (a bargain then!) and about five hundred a year in repairs, total £3200. Divide that by five, that's just over £600 a year. That is cheap motoring. That car new was £23,000! The person who drove it out of the showroom lost about four grand as they went into the street. Depreciation on any new car will set you back more than £600. It can pay handsomely to buy good quality secondhand goods.

Buying well behind the market, you can enjoy the benefits of wonderful things you could not afford to buy new.

Even if I had the money, I would always choose to buy well kept secondhand expensive objects, and save the rest for a rainy day.

SELL YOURSELF - HOW? BE CONCERNED ABOUT YOUR CUSTOMERS!

One basic principle is often overlooked when selling:

> **Certainly the product is important, but the most important thing you ever sell is yourself.**

What that means in practice is we need conduct ourselves in ways that makes people like us. So how? Be interested in them. Listen to them. That is the secret.

WHEN YOUR BUSINESS BUILDS, AS SOON AS YOU CAN - GET HELP!

Many people, fed up with working for somebody else, decide they will not work for a tyrannical, mean, critical, impatient, intolerant boss who demands they work all hours there are, and then some, and never pays overtime. So they become self-employed.

Are their problems over? Not on your life! They find they now have a new tyrannical, mean, critical, impatient, intolerant boss who demands they work all hours there are, and then some, and never pays overtime, and now there is no escape. Their new boss is themselves!!!

It takes a lot of hard work, sweat, toil, and yes some tears to get a new business going. Even if you have discovered the proverbial "better mousetrap", and people are beating a path to your door, you have a hard row to hoe. Pretty soon, the new "boss" (You!) is working all hours, trying ineffectually to keep up with all the paper work, the telephone calls, the ordering, the packing and mailing, and the thousand and one jobs that running any business seems to involve. So as soon as you are earning enough to keep yourself, think about getting some help.

"I CAN'T POSSIBLY AFFORD IT!!!!" I hear you scream. "I can barely make ends meet as it is."

Right, that is the trap almost everyone falls into. It is painful in a trap, ask any mouse. So it is best to see the trap coming, and circumnavigate it if you can. And you can.

How? Well, what is your time worth to you? Supposing you are making five pounds an hour for your time after costs and expenses. There are plenty of people, like high school children, pensioners, and others who would be grateful to have a job a few hours a week that paid £2-3 an hour.

Remember a most important point. Money you pay to someone else is a business expense, and can be deducted from your profit. So in fact that £3 per hour is only costing you £2.25. Twenty-five percent is paid back by the government in tax relief.

So get someone in to do the packing, or the filing, or any mundane jobs that tie you down and prevent you from doing more profitable things that will expand your business.

You will be less tired, make better decisions, and pretty soon you will be making more money.

Then you can have them work a few more hours a week. This will free you up more to do the important things that they cannot possibly do, such as planning the growth and development of your business, formulating goals, writing to-lists. Like selling your services or products, or negotiating with suppliers for better prices and delivery.

This is the first step in building an expanding business. Many self-employed people never make this first step. They are tied down to the hamster wheel of business and work trivia which exhausts them.

You may not have so much money initially, but within a very short period, if you spend the time you have freed up for yourself wisely, it will enable you to bring in more money. You will quickly be back to where you were, and probably, better off.

I started using help when my correspondence, my mailing list and accounts started taking too much of my time. I took on someone part time. I also used a pensioner to stuff envelopes and stick stamps on which is a very time consuming process.

Once you are overworking, driving yourself into an early grave, there is no other way for you to survive and grow, except by having others help you. So employ others intelligently to free you up, and take the pressure off you. Then the more you make, the more help you can afford, so you can earn even more. But only if you make the best use of your time.

If you ever do find yourself with some spare time on your hands in a quiet spell, fill those minutes with productive work. Make few phone calls, or address some envelopes. Ten direct mail shots a day is fifty a week which is 2500 a year. They WILL produce more business. Or maybe write out an ACTION to-do or immediate goal list. Anything but waste time. Sow seeds instead.

SPECULATE TO ACCUMULATE

This ancient piece of wisdom says: Spend in order to gain. Money under the mattress is dead money. In a sense it has no value, only a potential value if it is ever used. To be alive, money has to flow. It has to be given and received. Goods or services have to flow as a result of it. Business is a live flowing thing.

All the most effective ways to bring in more customers to your business cost money and time. So we need to spend money in order to buy new and continuing business. This helps ensure we have a steady flow and a growing income.

The skill is to decide the best ways to spend the resources you have at any one time. We need to think carefully and use our intelligence when we are spending money to expand. It does not take much savvy to understand the value of developing happy customers who become "Ambassadors". So it makes sense to spend part of your budget to get them.

Spending money on advertising can be like trying to fill a bucket with holes in it. There has to be some way to measure the effectiveness of your adverts. If you do not have a way to measure response, you may be better off spending your money in some other way.

EVERYTHING HAS TO MAKE A PROFIT

Make sure you have an adequate margin to cover your costs. If you are selling anything on at a discount, one rule of thumb is to take the unit cost, double it and then double it again. This gives you the retail price. Say an item costs £5. Double it to £10, and again to retail at £20. This gives you a good profit at retail, and still reasonable margin if you have to give a trade or other discount.

DON'T GIVE YOUR STUFF AWAY.

A great philosophy is to realize that unless Safeways or Chevron are giving away food and fuel at a loss or for nothing, you are not obliged to give your goods or services away, however "deserving" someone might appear.

They are huge companies, and perhaps they can afford to be charitable, but do not give in to pleas of those seemingly hard up, otherwise you will shortly find yourself on the dole. When you are sure you have made a profit on the year, then that may be the time to consider some type of charitable activity.

Watch your overheads. Know your break-even figure and watch it daily. Rent, rates, utilities, telephone, stamps, stationery, advertising can mount up. Especially cost out your mobile phone. It may get you business you would otherwise lose, but watch the cost per call.

SELL THE SIZZLE, OR THE TASTE, OR THE SMELL, OR THE FEEL....

You can talk about the ingredients of toffee until the cow's come home. You can explain the purity of the product for ever and a day. Giving someone a toffee to chew, experience that gush of saliva, and the tingle of the taste bud, and make all that conversation unnecessary. Cashmere jumpers are expensive, but once you have felt that wool, and even more seductively tried one on, you're hooked! (So unless you can afford the "gratification", don't even try it on!!)

It is essential to get your customers to be involved in a demonstration. Get them to experience what you do. Get them to taste it, feel it, smell it, touch it, hear it, but get their senses involved.

If what you do involves physical things or touch, make sure your prospect has a hands on demonstration. Give them the chance to experience the benefits in their own body. If you are offering something edible, get them to taste it. That is what it means to "Sell the sizzle!" Give excellent service. It is appreciated and you get fewer complaints.

POST SALES REASSURANCE

Most people, after they have made a major purchase, any significant commitment, or bought even a small item, often have some doubts. It's only natural. So it has to be only natural for us as business people of integrity and a genuinely concerned approach, to reassure that person and comfort them. We ask them if they think they have made the right decision. If they haven't, now is a good time to find out! You do not want to discover their doubts when they stop their payments, or cancel a cheque.

> **One really powerful tool for post-sales reassurance is to send a letter of appreciation to them after each sale, especially the first one.**

Make it a top priority to send each new client a thank-you letter. This does not apply if you are working in a sweet shop and selling bars of chocolate and crisps to hundreds of customers each day! But if you are selling anything of significant value, or if you want your client to continue with you, send them a thank you letter.

Tell them you hope they are happy with their purchase, or their decision to consult you. State that they are welcome to call you if they have any questions at all. Remind them that you offer a money back guarantee if they are dissatisfied in any way whatsoever. Invite them to come back to you again, unless they have already made an appointment to do so. If that is the case, state the day, date and time of the appointment in the thank-you letter. Tell them you are looking forward to seeing them, and serving them.

If you use a computer, it is so easy to keep a standard thank-you letter on file. Then after each new person has left, bring it up on to the screen and modify it slightly. Or better yet, have your assistant do it for you, if you have one. (And we do hope that you having an assistant is one of your priority goals!)

Ask your helper to modify the letter slightly so that it is personal to that person. All you have to do is change a sentence or two, adding a specific detail that could only apply to them. This makes for a much greater impact.

BE AWARE, EVERYONE KNOWS A LOT OF PEOPLE - SO KEEP CLIENTS HAPPY!

Everyone knows, or is acquainted or related to a number of people. Let us say it averages about one hundred individuals. If you do not think you know that many, start counting. Put a tick on a piece of paper, or better still, write down the name of everyone you speak to in a week, or over a month's time. Chances are, most of those people will have asked you how you are. They will give you an opportunity to tell them how you are feeling. Maybe if you have just had a bad experience with a salesperson, or a health practitioner, or anyone else, you might mention it to them in passing.

Supposing you know a hundred people, and you mention your bad experience to just ten of them. Those ten know a hundred people also, and mention what you said to ten of them. Within a day or two of your telling someone about this "rat" who treated you so badly, a hundred people may have heard about it!

Now think about one or more of your clients doing the same thing. It will not be long before hundreds of people in a month, and maybe thousands in the course of a year hear bad things about you! This will hurt your business.

On the other hand a "happy camper" can be your goodwill ambassador to dozens, hundreds or even thousands of people.

So make sure your clients are happy about their interaction with you. If you are the slightest bit suspicious that they are not, check. Ask them if they are happy. They will probably lie to you with a smile if they are not. But they might tell you if you draw them out in the right way. Especially if you have otherwise "sold" yourself to them.

You cannot afford to have even one or two really dissatisfied customers. This is especially in a small town where most people know each other, or know someone who knows someone...

Bear this in mind, if I upset this person, they might tell ten people, then a hundred or a thousand people will know about it.

ACCOUNTING AND RECORDS

Be warned! Most small businesses go bust in the first year. Learn as you go along exactly what your operating costs are. Know to a very fine margin how much your outgoing are. Keep adequate records.

The biggest single reason small businesses fail, is the lack of proper records. Keep a careful track of your purchases. Keep accurate stock records. You can buy both a secondhand computer, and a simple accounts programme for a very small outlay. This is one of the best investments you will ever make.

Keep your accounts up to date. Reconcile your bank statements each month the moment they arrive. Banks make mistakes. Keeping in the black is infinitely cheaper than going into the red.

PAY YOUR BILLS - AND SMILE!!!

Warning! Another reason why small businesses fail is because large businesses they supply dishonestly keep them waiting for their money. It is not that they do not have the funds to pay their suppliers, they withhold it. They keep people waiting three, four, five or six months on a thirty day account.

The small business if operating on a bank overdraft, may be precasiously hanging on by a thread. That delay in receiving the money due to them can cause them costs they cannot absorb, and bust they go.

The big company, the wealthy PLC, with an excellent cash flow situation, who should be ashamed of themselves at such lack of integrity of dealing, smiles and says in effect, "Tough, there is always someone else we can screw down in price to the last penny, and then pay them late, we could care less."

In a sense, we are stealing, if we do not pay our bills on time.

Tax authorities bills for instance carry an automatic interest penalty if they are paid late. So that tells us that if we pay anyone late, we are robbing them of the interest on their money.

Whatever size of business we are running, or whether we are a private individual, there is a spiritual law, yes a spiritual law, which says in effect, "Pay on the nail." Do not keep anyone waiting for their money when you have it in the bank or in your savings account. If you cannot afford to pay the bill, we should not have purchased the item in the first place. And that includes utilities like the telephone, the gas and the electricity bills.

Here is a proverb written about three thousand years ago. It is a living principle today also:

"Withhold not good from them to whom it is due, when it is in the power of your hand to do it.

Say not to your neighbour, (or debtor) Go, and come again, and tomorrow I will give it to you, when you have it by you!"

WHAT ABOUT PAYING TAX?

By the by, having mentioned the dreaded word "tax", there is a principle involved here too. The Bible does not give explicit detail about every aspect of our modern world, but there is a living law that covers every principle of our behaviour.

Christ said of taxes, pay "Caesar" first. He demonstrated to His disciples, that it is our privilege and responsibility to pay taxes.

Nobody likes to pay tax, but the truth is they are necessary. I am not saying that the taxation system is fair, or that the money is always wisely and properly spent. We can hardly grizzle at that, since we do not always spend our own money wisely either!

Since there is a need for everyone to pay tax, we may as well do it with good grace.

It is not good for us to carry around grudging or negative attitudes regarding anything, even tax! Since we all live together in villages, towns and cities, we call ourselves a society. We cannot afford individually to do everything for ourselves. The authorities need to have tax money, to pay for roads, street lighting, hospitals, pensions, police, the armed forces, and so on, individuals cannot do that.

We are quick to complain when the hospital in our area closes its Casualty Wing, or the Police are slow to answer emergency calls. Those things are paid for out of out taxes. If we paid no taxes, there would be no public facilities.

The stability of the country we live in depends on having a government that can authorise what is necessary at the local area, and nationally provide protection from those who might be tempted to bully our nation. So why not be a happy taxpayer. Understand what taxes are for, and be grateful for what they provide. It is not our responsibility to be concerned how taxes are spent, apart from our legal right to vote. How they are used is for the conscience, (if any) of the politicians to handle. They are in a unique position of not having to produce a set of accounts like the rest of us.

Well, what a happy note to end our dissertation on money. It is a good idea to review this and the other sections, as explained in the section on review. Money is an important topic, which is why we have devoted two sections to the subject.

So here is a review of the topics covered in the two sections on finances: To repeat for emphasis, review and memory, in the previous section on money we covered:

1. **MONEY MAKES THE WORLD GO ROUND.**
   If we did not have trade, then we would not be able to buy the goods and services we need.
2. It is wise to make financial independence one of your primary goals:
   a. You don't waste valuable energy worrying about bills.
   b. You can spend your time more productively
   c. You develop beneficial character traits.
   d. You learn to live within your means.
   e. You work from a position of strength to help others
3. Live within your means
4. Avoid the trap of so-called "easy money".
5. Become a millionaire, or at least well-off by saving.
6. Avoid "Instant Gratification".
7. Spend now - Pay later is absolute folly.
8. Watch out for credit cards, interest is wasted money.
9. Learn "Delayed Gratification", the opposite of buy now-pay later.
10. Save money, be your own "loan shark".
11. Buying a home and taking on a mortgage.
12. Beware of being a guarantor.
13. If you are employed, make yourself indispensable.
14. Think about starting/developing your own business, however small.
15. Stay with what you know
16. Have Faith, Confidence, and Belief in your Products Services and Ideas.

In this section we covered:

- Sowing seeds to grow your business
- Success in life is a numbers game.
- Expand your contacts, sell yourself to as many people as possible.
- Sell yourself, or be concerned about the welfare of your customers.
- As your business builds, get help!
- Speculate to accumulate.
- Everything has to make a profit.
- Sell the sizzle, or the taste, the smell, or the feel...
- Post sales reassurance.
- Be aware, everyone knows a lot of people for your good or ill.
- Accounting and records.
- Pay your bills and smile.
- Pay your taxes and smile too!

In our next section we will be looking at that elusive quality and characteristic of being happy.

≈ SUCCESS ≈

CHAPTER ELEVEN

HAPPINESS IS AN ATTITUDE OF MIND + POSITIVE ACTION

HAPPINESS IS AN ATTITUDE OF MIND + POSITIVE ACTION

Attitude is the most important word in the English language. Our attitude determines everything we do in life. Everyone wants to be happy, but it is elusive and transient. Why are we not happy? How can we generate a measure of happiness for ourselves, and for others on an ongoing basis?

Happiness does seem to be an aspect of life that is rather difficult to define. In some ways, the harder people strive after that "happiness" they want, the more it seems to escape them.

> **Chasing "happiness" in a vague sort of wishful thinking way is about as ineffective as seeking a pot of gold at the end of the rainbow.**

There are no pots of gold to be found at the non- existent, elusive "end of the rainbow". Pots of gold are only accumulated as a result of working in harmony with the eternal laws of success, studying hard, accumulating ideas and producing values for others.

People often jest saying, "Money doesn't bring happiness, but at least you can be miserable in comfort!" Many people have given energy to the notion that owning things like cars, houses and power boats can make one happy.

You only have to consider the miserable lives of some of the rich and famous.

Wealthy people who have all too often ended their lives rather than continue in their misery. All the trappings of success and wealth failed to give them the inner happiness they sought.

Happiness is not to be found by happenstance, or by accident. Happiness is a result of living life in a certain way. For every cause there is an effect. Let us look at some of the ways we might produce the value we call "happiness". We want to have some for ourselves, and certainly we would like to be able to spread a little to other people we know and care about.

SHORT TERM INDUCED "HAPPINESS"
Temporary "happy" feelings may be experienced as a result of watching an uplifting film, or a good play, or by reading a well written book. The happiness we experience as a result of these activities is a by-product of the study, ideas, and values that someone put into those artforms.

The satisfaction and joy the producers, the directors, and the authors derived from making the film, the play or writing the book, are eternal values that are capable of producing a measure of happiness and joyfulness in others.

Although happiness gained in such ways can yield a degree of satisfaction, there is nothing to beat the type of happiness that is produced by your own achievements, and spiritual development.

People sit around and wish they were happy.
They blame their lack of money, the scarcity of entertainments
in their area, the way they are treated by other people and so on.
Rather than act, and take responsibility for their own state of mind.

It is certainly true that having insufficient funds to pay the bills, or not having much in the way of facilities where you live, or keeping company with negative people are not conducive to happiness.

However, sitting around and bemoaning these facts is not going to help much to produce happy feelings either! If we are not happy, then it is because we are not in harmony with the eternal laws that will produce a continuing measure of deep satisfaction of which happiness is a by-product.

The laws that produce internal joy may be intangible, but the manner in which they affect our lives is very real. So what are some of the ways we might set about producing some happiness in our lives? Before we consider those things which will make ourselves internally happy from day to day, we can look at a few things which will bring a moment of happiness to others first.

MAKING OTHERS HAPPIER HELPS US FEEL HAPPIER

One of the most effective ways to replace our own miserable feelings with those of joy, is to do something to, or for someone else that makes them feel happy.

> **Few people have more real friends than they have fingers on one hand.**

One way to build and develop friendships is to communicate with people in a positive way on a regular basis.

Perhaps you might send someone a card with a happy positive message. Cards can be expensive, and if you are not particularly flush at the moment, a sheet of paper is inexpensive. So how about writing a note to someone who you know needs some encouragement at this time? Picture them smiling at the nice things you are saying to them. Visualize them getting pleasure from your card or note, and yes, a little happiness too. Lo and behold, you get to feel some reflected happiness too! Perhaps telephone a friend, first being sure that you have something positive and happiness producing to say!

If you get onto the phone merely to share the way YOU are feeling at the moment, i.e. miserable, or at least not particularly happy, then do not make the call until you have gathered your thoughts for a moment, and thought of something positive and useful to say.

If you cannot think of anything happy making, ring them up anyway and ask how their day went. Just LISTENING to someone else can help them to have some joy, and a little of their joy will splash over onto you as well. Even if they had a rotten day, you're listening, and your words of sympathetic encouragement may just be what makes the difference for them to handle tomorrow better. And, you will feel happier with yourself for doing it.

If someone you know did anything that counts as an achievement, then "Congratulations!", or "Well done!", or "Great stuff!" will send a ray of happiness into your friend's heart. Ask them for more details, and as they explain what they did, you can enjoy it too. None of us really receive enough sincere appreciation of the things we achieve in life, whether little or large. Being warmly commended can create a really wonderful feeling of internal happiness.

A friend of mine I have known for many years habitually says to me, "You deserve that", or "You worked hard for that result." I know it is always sincerely meant, and emanates from the warmth and joy that they are feeling towards me. And that makes me feel better if I am at all down.

How about sending some flowers, or a small gift. The happiness a gift brings is not necessarily proportionate to its cost. I have received some very inexpensive items over the years which made me very happy when I received them. Some presents, like a can opener or a screwdriver, which cost only a few pounds at most, have continued to give me great pleasure every time I use them. They also serve to remind me of the happiness a certain person gave me at the time.

By the way, we are not surprised to receive presents at Xmas or on birthdays or other special "events" in people's lives, it is the norm. But, little gifts that come at unexpected times, and for no apparent reason, can bring a disproportionate amount of happiness and joy to the recipient. As they say it is not the cost, but the thought that counts. Their joy increases your joy.

Give someone a tip BEFORE they give you the service. They will enjoy it, and you will be very happy with the extra service you will receive. Everyone gets a little happiness.

ENSURING WE HAVE A STEADY SUPPLY OF "HAPPY"

What is the best source of a continual flow of happy feelings? Without question, it is a steady stream of genuine personal accomplishments. They do not have to be major accomplishments either. Simply writing a long overdue letter, or tidying your desk at long last, or finally oiling that squeaky hinge.

Notice the thread that runs through that list. It is the joy we get from doing something we have put off doing. Procrastination is said to be the thief of time. It is also the thief of happiness. If putting things off builds guilt, regret, and lowers self-esteem, then getting them done does the opposite.

It is impossible to feel guilty about getting something done.

You cannot regret achieving something worthwhile

And you cannot feel badly about yourself if you have just been successful at something. Get started on the smallest things. Make a list of all those things you have put off, and put off until you feel badly about them. When you have your list, lo and behold you have a list of GOALS. Small, tiny, maybe seemingly insignificant goals, but goals nevertheless.

So have we stumbled in a slightly different way onto another key to happiness, wealth and success? Indeed we have. Goalsetting implies that there are things we want to achieve. Without some sort of goal oriented action in our lives, the chances are that we will spend more time drifting than achieving. Certainly even without formally setting goals, we get things done each day. The unhappy fact is that we will probably be like the majority, living by accident.

We will be merely responding to the demands life makes on us, rather than working towards achieving the results of the demands we are making of life. These are two very opposite ways of living our lives. Striving after those goals that inspire us, creating ACTION To-Do lists, is a positive plan for happiness production. When we systematically get one thing done after another, this will inevitably cause us to be happier. Happiness is produced in greater and more long-lasting measure by our accomplishing things we thought worthwhile, and actively decided to do, than in any other way.

SELF-DISCIPLINE INCREASES PRODUCTIVITY

We were born to be productive beings. In a sense we are creators. We forge our own pathways in life. We either make ourselves miserable neglecting the laws of success, by indolence and laziness, or just drifting down the stream of life. On the other hand we make ourselves happier and happier as we achieve our purposes in life, by working in a disciplined way at accomplishing a series of minor successes.

Discipline in our modern society is almost a bad word. Yet without discipline, Chris Chataway would never have run the four minute mile, Sir Edmund Hilary would never have climbed Everest, nor would the American astronauts have put a foot on the moon. It takes discipline to order our lives. It takes strength of mind and purpose to get some things done, when we would rather take the easy way out and watch TV or a video.

Discipline is mental muscle. Muscles are built over a period of hard work and regular exercise whether on the job or in a gymnasium.

> **Mental discipline comes from lifting many tiny jobs off the procrastination list, and doing mental pressups until they are done.**

Each time we exercise our pathetically weak mental muscles, they get a tiny bit stronger. In exactly the same way as biceps or quadriceps muscles, if that exercise is not continued on a regular basis the muscles begin to diminish. So does the strength of our mental resolve and discipline weaken when we do not exercise them.

Practice on small, light easy mental tasks first. Get used to doing them first before you take on life-changing weighty decisions. If you try to bench press one or two hundred pounds the first time you go to the gym, you will probably be unsuccessful, and this will reduce your self-esteem and make you miserable.

If you press sixty pounds this week, sixty five next week and keep up a steady progress, you will eventually press the one or two hundred and feel marvellous, and happy at your achievement. So the skillful way to produce happy feelings is to build on a lot of small but useful successes. You will derive a little joy and happiness from each one. If you are constantly doing things that make you happy, it follows that the amount of time you feel miserable decreases in proportion.

AESTHETIC APPRECIATION

In our rushed, materialistic, modern way life, it is all too easy to neglect our inner spirit. This world for all its sadness, human woes, famines, wars, and man's inhumanity to man, is still a wonderful and a beautiful place. In a city environment it may be harder to get in touch with the beauty in nature, but it can be done.

Even looking up between the tall buildings at the sky when it is a nice day, or taking a moment to appreciate the wind or the softness of the rain, can be restorative and produce a sense of happiness. We induce a degree of happiness when we seek to enjoy the wonders of nature. There is joy to be had by the bucketful from a sunset, or the crashing of the waves on the seashore, or the wind in the willows, or the patterns of the water as it flow sparkling around the pebbles in the stream.

It is all too easy to lose sight of our amazing ability to appreciate lovely things. When we feed our minds on the lovely, the beautiful, the wondrous, we are uplifted in spirit. Our present day so- called civilised world, and way of life tends to stifle this side of us if we are not conscious and aware of our need to fight against materialism and the downside of society.

ENCOURAGING AND FEEDING THE HIGHER SELF

As we said earlier, the key to everything in life is "attitude". Human nature does not always naturally focus on the positive, the harmonious and the lovely. Our tendency as human beings is to spiral downwards, with the emphasis on our lower selves. We get greedy, aggressive, selfish, unkind, impatient, angry at the drop of a hat. These negative values all mitigate against our capacity for happiness and maintaining a joyful state of mind.

It takes a constant amount of work on our "attitudes" to preserve a daily progress towards engaging in positive values. It takes vigilance to do those things which are uplifting to our spirits. It takes guts and determination to go against the flow and the downward pull of negative people around us. It is not easy to work on ourselves daily. It is sometimes quite hard to be aware enough to make the positive decisions necessary to reject the pull of our lower selves. We need inner strength to foster the reactions, approaches and activities that will enhance our aspirations to develop spiritually.

> **We need to develop the habit of encouraging ourselves to develop the positive values which will give strength to our higher selves.**

It takes work to be peaceful, unselfish and altruistic, kind and patient. It takes self-control not to get angry every time something in life does not exactly suit us. One way to feed the spirit in a positive way is to read books by writers who have a gift for producing inspiring and uplifting material. Another is to look at true art which can do the same thing. "Modern art" does not always do this.

It is important to guard the doors of our minds. We receive, often unwittingly, scenes and visual images on the TV, in films, newspapers and magazines which it would probably better to avoid. There are certainly more forms of "entertainment" depicting violence and the degrading activities people indulge in than ever before. If we are seeking true abiding happiness, it is wise to exclude as much of this type of influence from access to our minds as is humanly possible.

There is another sinister problem surrounding us which is having an unrealized negative effect on us. Music is capable of being one of the highest forms of healing for our beleaguered spirits. It seems that the idea of music being melodic, harmonious, having a rhythm in balance, and a structure that is elegant, is all but vanished from the audio world.

People dressed in black, illuminated by migraine inducing flashing lights, mouth and scream obscenities into microphones to the backing of deafening cacophonous dissonant sounds, almost drowned by an ear shattering rhythm. They no longer have a structure, when they want to stop, they simply turn down the volume! It is now less easy to find beautiful, heartwarming, spiritually uplifting music, and it is out there. We just have to work a little harder to find it.

GETTING THE MIND TO FLOURISH AND PRODUCE FRUITS OF SUCCESS

Growing the "fruits of success" usually starts slowly at first just like a vegetable garden. Initially you have to clear away some of the bad habit "weeds" in your mental plot. Then plant the "seeds" of change, new approaches, ideas and practices. Then by mentally hoeing the fertile soil of your mind with repetitive positive action, the "Seeds of Success" will begin to germinate.

> **As your new garden of positive thoughts and productive ideas grows, you will begin to enjoy the fruits of a different harvest in your life.**

Instead of unhappiness, you will experience a new joy. Instead of poverty, you will welcome the gradual, slow but steady improvement in your financial positions. Instead of broken relationships, you will forge new and better links with those you want to have as part of your life.

Let us look at some of the ways our minds can stifle any happy feelings we might otherwise enjoy.

START WITH A MENTAL SPRING CLEAN

Each year, both we and our homes benefit from a good clear out. Getting rid of all the accumulated junk makes the whole place feel different. It also seems to clear the mind for action when the clutter has gone. The mind has more effect on the body and on our lives than anything else. A cluttered mind produces congested thinking and therefore muddled action. Our minds definitely function better in a neat and tidy environment.

To make significant changes in our lives we need to get rid of our "mental detritus". What is "mental detritus"? It is the mental equivalent of the physical foecal matter we void every day in the toilet. Unless we get rid of the waste by-products of what we eat regularly, we poison ourselves. Unless we get rid of the mental equivalent, which is negative and harmful thinking, we can never truly be happy.

What type of "mental detritus" poisons the mind? Here are a few types of thinking that cloud our mental processes:

Negative thoughts: I can't. It won't work. I'm no good at that.
Regrets: I wish I had.. I should have... If only I had...
Hates: Pet hates we dwell on. Ain't it awful thoughts.
Resentments: That wasn't fair. Life isn't fair. You hurt me...
Unrealistic fears: I might fail. Fear of failure. Fear of success!
Bad attitudes: Procrastination - the thief of time. Guilt.
Taking on too much. Laziness. (Definition: Working hard doing what you want to do instead of what you ought to do to build a new, prosperous, efficient life.) Critical of others: Analyze, maybe. Criticise - no.

Gossiping: Telling tales to other people about those you know.
Dishonesty: Lying. Deceiving. Misrepresenting.

Self-martyrdom: Excessive self-sacrifice. Poor me-ing. Self-centeredness.

That'll do for a start. Examine yourself to see what your specialty bad attitudes are. Maybe write a list of those that plague you. We are all different. Then start working systematically to eliminate them. When you clear a garden of weeds, if you do not put plants in the space, the weeds just come back. So as you rid yourself of the mental garbage ways of thinking, replace them with positive thoughts. Catch yourself as you allow your mind to go its own old destructive way. Stop yourself from expressing the negative attitudes that have historically held you back. One of the best ways to do this is to read some of this material and listen to one of these tapes every day. If not this programme, then another that will uplift you and give you the mental nourishment you need today to be happy.

Listen in your car going to work. Or buy a quality walkman, and listen to them in any short break you might have. The positivity will recharge your mental batteries and keep the negativity at bay.

PICTURE WHAT YOU REALLY WANT!

If what you want is available in magazines, but some, or better still get some old ones for nothing that someone else has finished with. Then cut out the glossy coloured pictures of what you want. Get a cork board, and display them in a place in your home where you can look at them regularly. Put one on the back of your toilet door so that you have something positive to look at while you are getting rid of the old stuff!

Visualization works! If you visualize negative things, then that is what you produce. If you focus on picturing positive changes in your life, then that is what you will bring to yourself.

Three factors in maintaining a mental growth posture:
1. Have a hobby that you really enjoy.
2. Have a project that excites you.

Learning is a lifelong process, you may as well find something you enjoy learning about!
3. Take any opportunity to speak confidently in public.

If the prospect of giving a talk terrifies you, we have a course on it. We also offer personal consultations to get you over the fear in five minutes. Yes, five minutes! Guaranteed, or your money back!!

President Abraham Lincoln said: "I will prepare, for some day my chance will come." Pray that your chance will not come until you ARE ready! When it does come, be happy!

HAPPINESS INCREASES PRODUCTIVITY AND WEALTH
Think BIG - and be happy to start small. Take one step at a time. Success by the inch is a cinch! ### Absolute fundamental law: Them as gets - gets more!

Every time by your determined efforts, thoughts, plans and actions, you add to your knowledge, you're "Prosperity Capital Account", to your possessions, or whatever, a magic occurs.

You attract to yourself further increase. How? I do not know. It just happens. What form this will take is not always clear, but something will come to you.

1. WANT your aim with a passion.
2. Do something, however small, to take you a step towards achieving your goal.
3. Increase your desire by picturing it with interest and enthusiasm, in glorious technicolor.
4. When it starts to happen, revel in it, and get happy!!

Remember, in life, you either are going forward to fulfillment of one thing or another; or you are slipping back into mediocrity only to vegetate. There is no way to escape the inevitable results of natural law. Break them and they break you. Get in harmony with them - and you succeed.

Affirmations help. "I have all the money I want. I have plenty of money in my pockets, my bank account, or readily available for my use." Believe this strongly enough and your whole approach to life will change. You may think it is a nutty idea, I challenge you to do it for a year. Then write to me and tell me that it did not work at all. I won't hold my breath for your letter.

But supposing you are broke. Then picture yourself in the future being able to say the above truthfully. You will be sowing seed of prosperity in your brain no matter how poverty stricken you might be at the moment. By all means avoid poverty statements like: "I can't afford it", or "I've never got enough money". They are death to prosperity. Replace them with statements like, "When I have money for that project, I will go ahead with it", or "When the time is right, the funds for that will materialise".

Great success and happiness are founded on the law of many minor achievements. Hundreds of little successes produce happiness, and wealth as a by-product.

FINDING HAPPINESS IN LOVE AND TRUE VALUES
Nobody will suggest that it is easy to love. It may not be easy, but it is the only worthwhile way to live. It is amazing that the English language has only one word to express so much. The Eskimos have eight hundred words for snow, we have only one for love. Yet there are more shades of meaning of the word LOVE than there are of snow.

Love has to be defined by other powerful words. The beautiful building love can become, has to built on sure undergirding foundations. If the foundations are allowed to erode, the beautiful temple of love that can be built between two people, or neighbours, or countries, or races, will crumble.

FOUNDATIONS TO BUILD HAPPY, LOVING RELATIONSHIPS ON RESPECT
Respect is the first essential foundation. It involves honouring the right of the individual to be who they are. It implies consideration,

esteem, and honour. Also to refrain from interfering with another's privacy or right to live the way they do, and avoid forms of control and criticism in communication.

ACCEPTANCE

It is a lovely feeling to be completely accepted by another. To know that it is all right to be who you are, all the time, in every circumstance. It is not easy to accept someone just the way they are. It does not involve agreeing with or approving of all they do. It means not judging them. To the extent our feelings towards another depend upon whether they match the way we would like them to be, this is not love. It is an imposition of our mind-set upon them. The result is always destructive.

COMMUNICATION

Free, open, caring, clear communication is essential. It is vital that any subject be open to discussion in full. Only of course with the foundation of respect and acceptance.

We cannot read the mind of others, and so to tell them what they think, or mean, or feel, is truly counter productive in any loving relationship.

IT TAKES TWO

Unless both parties in any loving relationship agree on the need for the foundations of Respect, Acceptance and Communication, love cannot grow.

Where love reigns, mistakes are either overlooked, meekly endured, or speedily forgiven, so that notwithstanding the imperfections of those who live together, they bear with, and make the best of each other; and peace and harmony are preserved.

JOYFUL LOVE - THE OPPOSITE OF THE MISERY OF INFATUATION

Love is the quiet understanding and mature acceptance of imperfection. It is real. It gives you strength and grows beyond you

- to bolster your beloved. You are warmed by their presence, even when they are away. Miles do not separate you. Love is a friendship that has caught fire. It takes root and grows - one day at a time. Love says: "Be patient. Don't panic. Your partner is truly yours. Plan your future with confidence." Love is the maturation of friendship. It is important to be friends, before you are lovers, not the other way around. Love involves trust. You are calm, secure, and unthreatened. Your partner feels that trust and responds by being more trustworthy. Love makes you look up. It makes you thing up. It makes you a better person than you were before.

LOVE IS... THE WAY TO TRUE HAPPINESS

Love CAN be defined. Because it is such big subject, it needs many many words adequately to describe all aspects of love.

Quite a lot is talked about being "spiritual". Quite what it means in real terms is rarely spelt out. It is the pursuit of positive values. There are qualities of spirit which define upbuilding spiritual attributes, that build character, and produce true happiness. So dwell on joy, peace, calm, tranquility, patience, long-suffering, gentleness, strength of purpose, and be happy.

This book has not devoted any space to any religion for good reasons. The author has written several books on Theology as opposed to religion. So, what is Theology? It is the study and application of the Bible laws and principles. It is God's Instruction Book for His Children to read in order to have His guidance in their lives.

Human beings all over the world choose to believe in ridiculous lies like a fictitious 'Mother Nature' which of course does not exist. They observe with intensity, Christmas, Easter, Halloween, and other outright pagan practices, while ignoring God the Father and His Son the Creators of all things.

People who several times a day acknowledge God and thank Him for Life, for every heartbeat and breath, are in a very different position to live a life of Wealth Health and Happiness than those who do not. We have learned that we have the responsibility of CHOICE and to CHOOSE our spiritual attitude and frame of mind.

To summarize in review:

- Happiness is an attitude of mind + positive action.
- Get some short-term induced happiness from good books and art.
- Making others happy, helps us feel happier.
- Ensure we have a continuous supply of "happy" through accomplishments.
- Self-discipline increases productivity and therefor happiness.
- Get happiness from aesthetic appreciation.
- Encourage and feed the higher self with spiritual values.
- Springclean and weed the mind to grow the fruits of success.
- Picture what you really want, and be happy when you get it!
- Happiness increases productivity and wealth.
- Finding happiness through love and the true values.
- Relationships built on Respect, Acceptance, and Communication are sound, and it takes two.
- Love as opposed to infatuation.
- Love is the way to true happiness.

CHAPTER TWELVE

HERE'S TO YOUR WEALTH, HEALTH AND HAPPINESS

Here are some additional thoughts on creating a better life for yourself, with more prosperity, better health and more happiness.

TO BE WEALTHY - THINK BIG, BUT START SMALL

People often fail to reach the heights of which they are truly capable because they do not think big enough. Picture yourself enjoying being successful in places that are of high quality with people of achievement.

TO BE WEALTHY - DEVELOP THOUGHTS AND THINKING POWER

"Think and grow rich", said Napoleon Hill. He was right.

You are not what you think you are, but what you think you become. Mental stretching is good for the mind. Explore new ideas.

What you are thinking today will determine the level of your activity a year from now.

Your aren't really thinking like a millionaire until you act like one. You cannot act like a millionaire until you think like one!

Thoughts are transient, but they have a life. Thought forms which are constantly reinforced have a longer life, and they traverse the globe.

Understand the value of a dry run. Test it out. Be conscious and acknowledge the necessity of rehearsal. Rehearsals are necessary to attain perfection. The value of a dress rehearsal is to have all the pieces in place, and to make sure it will work on the night.

THINK WEALTHY - OPEN A "PROSPERITY ACCOUNT"

Count your cash on hand. If you have not already done so, one specific action that will help to propel you on your way, is to open a special "Prosperity Account" with whatever you can afford, leave it in there and don't touch it, even if it is only ten pounds.

Plan to increase this "Prosperity Account" on a daily basis, even if it is only by one penny. You do not have to pay such small sums into the bank or savings account, but have a place to keep this money. Do not touch it for any reason, except to pay it in.

It is not your petty cash jar. If you want one of those, have one, but keep it separate from your "Prosperity Account" We have discussed this in detail in the section on money and finances, but we mention it here, with the suggestion, if you have not yet done it, to get this started right away, without delay.

TO BE WEALTHY - WATCH YOUR UNTOUCHABLE SAVINGS GROW

Hopefully by now, you have started saving the 10% you will never touch. You are exercising the discipline of "Delayed Gratification" so you will have wealth to fall back on in your later years. It is exciting to see that account grow, slowly at first, but surely, year by year. Congratulations for actually doing it. Give yourself a pat on the back, and put your self-esteem up at least two notches.

BECOME PROSPEROUS - OPEN A "CAPITAL ACCOUNT"

Another account you may want to open is the "Capital Account" This is money to fund your enterprises. Again it does not matter how small the amount, to start with. Say you could only manage to put a pound away in this account. Put it into an empty jar which you have labelled "Capital".

Create your own risk/financing capital. Be your own loan shark! Remember, there is no legitimate offer that will no still be there tomorrow, unless someone else got there first!

BUILD YOUR CAPITAL FOR WEALTH, HEALTH AND HAPPINESS

What could I possibly do with only a pound? If nothing else you might go to a garage sale, and walk around twice looking at everything with one thought in mind, "Could I buy that for a pound and sell it for two, or at an even greater profit?"

Yes, there is usually a lot of junk in garage sales, and you can pick up some nice things for next to nothing. Recently, I happened to be attending a large one with a friend of mine who runs an antique shop. I saw a brand new pair of Adidas sports shoes. They were marked £1.50. I said, "Would you take a pound?" The lady replied, "Yes." I handed over my pound.

Now these shoes were new, and would have cost at least thirty or forty pounds. So I took them home and put £20 in my "Capital Account" from my money I had received as income. Does that sound crazy? Well, here is my reasoning. If I had gone to a shop and bought those shoes, I would have had to pay a lot more than £20 for them out of my already tax paid income. I needed the shoes, they were not a luxury.

So having bought them for a pound, I "sold" them to myself for a 2000% profit, and put the money into my "Capital Account" so that when I next see something that I can resell at a profit, I now have £20 capital instead of £1. Of course I could have chosen to put those shoes "in stock", and sold them to someone else at my sports club at a profit. The amount of profit would have depended upon the price another sports person was willing to pay for them, but it would certainly be much more than a pound. I would then have put the proceeds into my "Capital Account", but I needed them myself. This is a true story, except that my "Capital Account" has a great deal more in it than just one pound.

So you might say, "What on earth are you bothering about, all that trouble for a pound, and you certainly did not need the £20 if you have so much in your "Capital Account". That may be true, but it is a matter of great importance for me to keep operating the trading profit principle. How do you think I got all that money in the account? It was from starting small, and gradually building it up.

BE WEALTHIER - EXPECT TO WIN. TEN WAYS TO PREPARE
1. Positive preparation.
   Have plans and contingency plans of how you want things to turn out. Use the positive affirmations to counter any negative thoughts that might creep in unawares. Affirmations without discipline is frequently delusion.
2. Anticipation.
   Practice anticipating all the good that is going to come your way. If you do not expect to win, to grow and to develop, you won't. Think and anticipate success on a daily basis.
3. Be alert for new ideas.
   Avoid rejecting new ideas out of hand. Avoid jumping into new ideas. Sort them carefully.
   Don't be caught with "fools gold", learn what the real thing looks like and find nuggets of gold.
4. Exploration
   Make an agreement with yourself only to explore possibilities cautiously, and with the idea in mind, "Will this help me progress towards my purpose and my goals?"
5. Be Empathetic
   Be as concerned about others needs and wants, as you are about your own. This helps us watch for trends. Catching a trend is like a surfer catching a wave, the energy is free, but only for as long as it lasts, then it is time to look for something else.
6. Don't blame others, take responsibility yourself.
7. Take life as it comes with fortitude and determination.
   If things suddenly look like they are going to go your way, it might pay to drop other distractions and focus on that project.
8. Take a long-term view.

We are living in a TIME of rush. The demands of the immediate moment are pressing. It is imperative to force spaces into the schedule to allow for long-term thinking.

9. Don't allow yourself to get "carried away".
   A "feet on the ground" approach will serve you well when others are indulging flights of fancy, spending time and money appealing but useless projects.
10. TEST, TEST, TEST, or DON'T BE AFRAID TO START SMALL.

Before you put your shirt on an idea, or project, test is out on a few people. Get the reaction of your future possible customers.

BE SUCCESSFUL
- Add at least one contact to your list every day.
- If it needs doing - do it now!
- Resist all high pressure offers.
- Be decisive when shove comes to push - do it.
- Know where you are going and go there.
- Know where people are going and help them to get there.

BE HEALTHIER - TWELVE WAYS TO BUILD YOUR HEALTH
1. Have a sense or purpose and pursue it with intensity.
2. Drink pure water every day, at least four to six glasses.
3. Sit down quietly three times each day to a balanced assortment of fruits, vegetables and proteins. Buy the best food you can, organic if possible, eat some raw and cook some. Enjoy the colours and the flavours. Give thanks beforehand, and eat only when your mind is tranquil.
4. Rest. Give yourself regular short breaks of rest. Either vertical, sitting or lying down. A few minutes rest works wonders.
5. Enthusiasm. maintain a positive attitude and an enthusiasm for life. Find things to get reasonable happy, and excited about with restraint. Tell others what a great job they are doing. Tell

others how good they look, or how nicely they are dressed. Spread a little joy wherever you go.
6. Project. Project yourself, what you want, where you want to get to. Let others know how you are feeling about life, so long as it is positive and happy.
7. Work on improving your sense of humour. Look for fun in the ordinary things of life. Laugh with people about the oddities of life, never at them, or make humour at anyone else's expense.
8. Cultural attainments. A garden, a musical instrument, a new book, paint a picture. Expand your cultural self.
9. Develop your special skills. Never stop honing them.
10. Socialize with those whom you can uplift or those who uplift you. Build your libido with nutrients and supplements.
11. Exercise. Raise your resting heart rate to an appropriate level for ten minutes every day.
12. Take nutritional supplements ten days out of every fourteen. Build up your immune system with Vitamin A and Vitamin C. Fight the free-radicals with Vitamin E, Selenium, etc. Keep your energy levels up with blood sugar balancing Chromium, your brain sharp with Zinc and Gotu Kola or Ginkgo Biloba. Maybe consult a kinesiologist to have yourself nutritionally tested. It is very much worth the time and money spent.

BE HEALTHIER - HOW TO STAY YOUNG AND LIVE LONGER

When we are young, and in our twenties and thirties, we think we will live forever. If we are healthy, we take it for granted. We use and abuse our bodies, just as he mood takes us. Little thought is given to the long term need to nurture our bodies and look after our health.

So this section is an appeal. An urgent message for us to take care of our health while you have it. There is absolutely no need to get sicker as we get older. A steady deterioration in health might be the norm, but it most certainly does not need to happen.

There are habits which produce and maintain health and longevity if we will only apply them to our daily lives we will stay younger, healthier, and live longer.

HOW OLD ARE WE?

Our Chronological Age: The Greek word chronos means time. Our timer starts ticking the moment we take our first breath. We cannot alter how long we have been on this earth.

Our Imagined Age: Many people are obsessed with their age, and our perception of how old we are can be worked with and changed.

Our Psychological Age: We can be mature at aged twenty, or childish at forty-five and puerile at seventy, or the other way around. We can be wise when young, and wiser when we are older. That is what this programme is all about.

The more we study, and live our lives purposefully rather than by accident, the more mature we become. The power of the mind is virtually unlimited. Our minds can either be used powerfully to produce health and well-being and steady personal development, or it can be used negatively to destroy our health and cause us to deteriorate and degenerate both mentally and physically.

Our Anatomical Age: Over stressing our bodies either with mechanical work or overly zealous exercise programmes can actually age the anatomical body. A moderately exercised body which has not been subjected to undue strain will age less. Every time the long bones are flexed, it improves our immune system, so regular exercise helps keep disease at bay.

Our Physiological Age: The physiology of the body refers to how well the organs and the biochemistry of the body are working. A body well fed with good food, both raw and cooked in balance for that person will regenerate itself and keep itself young. The cells of our bodies are dying and being replaced all the time. We can either build new cells with good materials from excellent food and supplements, or eat junk foods and gradually produce a junk filled body. The choice is ours to make on a daily basis.

Our Actual Age: This is where all the components of ageing come together. How well we look after the structure, the internal organs, and how efficiently we guard and use our minds determines our actual age from day to day and from year to year.

BE HEALTHIER - EIGHT ROUTINES THAT AFFECT LONGEVITY

It is not much fun to live longer than the average person if we are sick, tired and miserable, and have lost all joy of living. Nobody wants to finish up in an old people's home to vegetate the last years of life. Do you? We have some control over how we age. So here are eight factors to watch:

1. Maintain a positive mental attitude.
2. Avoid smoking and secondhand smoke.
3. Avoid snacking, especially sugary one and sweet fizzy drinks.
4. Alcohol in moderation. A little seems to help longevity.
5. Eat only when hungry. Eat only good healthy food with gratitude. Chew all food until liquid.
6. Maintain body weight within 20% of the recommended norm.
7. Enjoy regular moderate exercise, raise heart rate for ten minutes a day to a safe level.
8. Avoid sleeping substantially more than seven hours a night.

BE HAPPIER - HOW TO STAY YOUNG AND LIVE LONGER

Here we offer twelve aspects of life which all help to ensure youthful longevity. People who have reached a healthy great age possess the following twelve attitudes of mind:

1. They have a clear sense of purpose. The most important factor, given that we have a positive attitude is to have a well-defined sense of purpose for our lives. This is why this is discussed in the very first part of this programme.

2. They have a good sense of humour.
3. They are optimistic and positive.
4. They are mentally active,
5. They manage stress well.
6. They have nutritious eating habits.
7. They exercise regularly.
8. They have a healthy libido.
9. They practice wise hygiene.
10. They are psychologically younger than their chronological age.
11. They have loving, honest, and supportive relationships.
12. They have no fear of dying. This is a big factor that needs attention. We all are born to die. It is futile to attempt to hide from this fact. It is destructive to fear death, either our own or that of others. Worrying about dying spoils our joy of living and should be dealt with. If you have a problem in this area, it would be wise to spend some time and money to address the issue. Practitioners of Kinesiology have many techniques which can address successfully both excessive fears about death, and also grief.

MATURITY OF MIND

When we can take a step back from ourselves and evaluate our level of maturity, we have indeed reached a level of maturity.

One measure is the degree we take personal responsibility for our lives. We are the way we are because we are the way we are. If we do not like it, then there is a need to change ourselves. Take a long hard look at the real you.

Am I defensive over things left undone. Am I feeling guilty because I am not taking full responsibility for the way things worked out? Do not allow others to put you into a defensive posture when they criticise you whether the criticism be fair or unfair.

Do I tend to blame others or circumstances for my failures? Do I indulge in costly bursts of temper or unbridled emotion? Do I lack self-reliance.

Do I have the tendency to think only of the present? Have I contracted the disease of egocentricity?

Do I lack a mature conscience?

Self-reliance is great when it is balanced with getting other points of view and help from others when it is needed.

BE HEALTHIER - TEN WORDS TO MEDITATE ON

Breath, Water, Nutrition, Sex, Exercise, Rhythm, Recreation, Regeneration your Spirit.

BE HAPPIER - USE THESE DYNAMICS WITH OTHERS

Here are some dynamic words which have great power:

- **Appreciation.** Make it a point to show appreciation for everything that is done for you. A note, flowers, a phone call, a card.
- **Consideration.** Realize that our liberties begin where the other person's ends. Consider the other person's feelings and views.
- **Inspiration.** Encourage others by bringing a little light into their day helps the world run more smoothly
- **Understanding.** Let others know that you understand what they are going through.

BE HAPPIER - ON THE SUBJECT OF RELATIONSHIPS
READ "I'M O.K. - YOU'RE O.K."

This marvellous, revolutionary book taught me to look at the population through different eyes. People are either Adults, Parents or Children, one at a time, any two, or all three almost in the same instant.

I have gained immeasurable value from being to assess which mode someone is in when I am talking to them. Without becoming an amateur psychologist, if someone is speaking in a childish way, then I know that for me to be in a parent's role probably will not work very well.

My aim in life is to deal with everyone straight on, adult to adult. It is not always possible, and when it gets to be any type of a problem, I extricate myself from the interchange.

GIVERS AND TAKERS

Another fabulously helpful concept came to me in the book, "Givers and Takers". It is a very useful thing to be able to see whether someone is coming from a giving or a taking position, and respond accordingly. Nobody really likes the idea of a "taker". Yet without them, givers would be hard put to find anything to complain about!

However, in my ideal world there would be no "takers" only "receivers". Givers and receivers. The problem with most chronic givers is that they do not know how to receive. The problem with receivers, they need to develop their desire to give a little more. We have all got a lot of work to do.

Another useful guideline from that book was that Givers are sexually attracted to Takers and vice versa. It is quite easy to see how that could take many relationships into stormy waters, only to crash on the rocks of an insoluble problem.

ON THE SUBJECT OF HAPPINESS

There is one huge stumbling block to blissful happiness that needs a mention. People want to be happy and they cannot understand why they are not. Well, here is one answer.

Most of us are addicted to one extent or another to having everything in life to work out the way we want it to. If we do not like the way things happen, we get emotional, negatively so. We get cross, irritable, moody, as soon as things do not suit us. We might hide it, suppress it, choke on it, but inside we fume!

There is a solution. Not an easy one, but a solution nevertheless. It involves the use of the technique of sublimation. Sublimation is turning one emotion into another. In the old days, the alchemists used to claim they could change quartz into gold. They couldn't, but they got everyone intrigued.

Well, we can turn bad emotions into fuel for happiness. How? Sublimation. How does it work.

People think there are two ways to handle negative emotion. Either EXPRESS it, or SUPPRESS it.

There are actually three ways. The third is to sublimate it. We can choose not to express or suppress, but to transmute the negative energy into a positive energy. To do that we exercise our greatest power, CHOICE, and choose not to react, but to relax and learn from the experience in a positive way. This immediately releases a degree of happiness. We will feel joy at having won over ourselves. Try it and see.

BE HAPPIER - EXPRESS GRATITUDE

Golden Words: Thank you and Congratulations. People like to be appreciated, and remembered. Gratitude is a great quality to work on in an ungrateful world. When things start going your way, it helps mightily to have a grateful attitude. Grateful that is, to whatever external power or God you believe in. Gratefulness is a spiritual trait which encourages you to be given more. That is the way it works.

Most people are not very grateful at all. Mostly they just complain when they do not have enough. If something good does come their way, they grizzle that it is not enough, or not quite what they wanted. Just be happy you are receiving something and foster a feeling of gratitude. You will feel happier, and you WILL receive more.

Here are a few suggestions:

1. I am grateful for all the good that comes my way.
2. I am really grateful for all the good things today.
3. I will be successful because I want what is right for me, my clients, my associates and those I love and care about.
4. I am being enriched in mind, body and spirit, and good things into my life with a spirit of gratitude.

BE HAPPIER - EXPECT GOOD THINGS TO HAPPEN AND THEY WILL.

A mindset of "Positive Expectancy" works wonders. Every time your wealth, whether is be in monetary, mental or spiritual terms, notice and allow it to reinforce your attitude of Positive Expectancy.

Be confident that you will grow, even when and especially when all the apparent evidence is to the contrary. This is an exercise in FAITH. Faith is something you have to have in something that hasn't happened yet. Faith is a tangible thing. You feel it and express it although what you have faith in, is yet to occur.

Retaining and maintaining this attitude of Positive Expectancy is not easy, nothing worthwhile is easy. It is good to remember that. It takes work to maintain that frame of mind. This is especially true if we are surrounded by negative people. Gradually change that, spend more time with positive people

CALL TO ACTION

Where did I go wrong all those years? I didn't act soon enough, effectively enough, or determinedly enough! I let things slide. I gave a lot of my life and my time away. I do not regret that at all. Although those were not the most financially productive years, I was building other treasures of mind and self- discipline.

You ARE going to learn from my mistakes, aren't you? You ARE going to start making some changes today, aren't you? Each time you listen to a tape, or read one of these chapters, make notes in your new organiser. Write an ACTION To-Do list on the topic it covers. Do this each time, since you will get something different out of each part every time.

Decide to attend one of our seminars on Life Skills. This way you will meet others of like mind. Maybe you will be able to do some networking, and make some new acquaintances, who may one day become friends. At the seminars you will also be refreshed and hopefully, re-inspired, recharged with enthusiasm.

We all need that. Especially in England. Especially if the sun has not shone for a while!

As you become more of what you want to be, and success begins to knock on your door, welcome it, expand into it, enjoy it. You DESERVE it. Oh! Yes you do. You pulled yourself out of the rut you were in, (We all get in them!) and got working on your own case.

After using and applying these concepts and practicalities in your life for a while, take stock again. Remember, you took stock of your life at the beginning, if you followed the suggestion, and did it. Well, look back on those old notes, and see how far you have come. Hopefully you will have a very pleasant surprise.

Notice your savings, and your capital account and how they have grown into quite respectable amounts. Review your attitude. Has it not changed enormously for the better? Of course it has!

Just a quiet word of warning. When you start really "getting there", watch out for your ego. An exaggerated idea of self- importance and lording it over others are not traits to be admired.

One thing about most people who are both financially and spiritually wealthy, is they are really really nice people. They exhibit the finer qualities. They have their human nature well trained and under control. They make everyone around them feel good about themselves, partly because they feel good about themselves.

IN YOUR WILDEST DREAMS - THINK THE IMPOSSIBLE DREAM

Think about all the things you would like to do in your wildest dreams. The Australia Opera House, a walk in the black forest, a Cruise, (No! NOT Tom!!) a black forest gateau, a chateau, the Grand Canyon, owning a power boat, a yacht, dinner at the Ritz, a night at the Savoy, visiting famous places, the Louvre, a Jaguar, a Porche or a Rolls, Niagara Falls, golf at St. Andrews, meet Pavarotti, go to the Rockefeller Museum, diamonds, Bang

& Olufsen's Highest of Fi, a country cottage, a place by the lake, a view of the mountains from your kitchen, whatever.

It's your dream, you fill in the pictures. Then reinforce them by writing them down. There you have another goal list! Dwell on your dreams often enough and you will find they will come true, and you'll be there! But only and if you act NOW.

In conclusion: Now, for a last few words of encouragement. We have shared a vast amount of information in these twelve sessions. The potential is there, it is what you do with it that counts.

Each nugget of an idea can be turned into a goldmine of success and achievement. Each gem of a principle can be polished into greater prosperity and wealth.

Each tool can be honed to keep your mind sharp and your body healthy into your mature years. Each pearl of wisdom can propel you into realms of joy and happiness you never thought possible.

≈ SUCCESS ≈

ARRIVE EARLY, BREATH, VISUALIZE, SMILE AND ENJOY

Finally, here is a short story that has brought me a lot of happiness. A downhill champion skier was asked the secret of his success, and the joie de vivre he always displayed.

He said, "I have a four point plan for everything I do in life. I use it for all individual events, business appointments, social occasions, or whatever."

We include it here for you to make it work for your happiness and success.

1. Start off early, and arrive early.
2. Once there, breathe in deeply and breathe out slowly, and as you do visualize and affirm the outcome I want.
3. Visualize exactly what you want. Use the mind to control the mind, do not allow it to drift aimlessly. Emotions are vital to the effectiveness of achieving goals. Relax into alpha-wave relaxation, visualize, get a clear mental picture that makes me feel emotionally positive.
4. Smile, enjoy yourself, and have fun. After all that is what life is all about. If we lose sight of the fact that life is a game, and get too serious, we will miss out on a lot of the pure enjoyment of this time we spend in the earthly school.

Well that concludes this section on happiness.

Now to summarize our programme by section:

In the first section we covered self-esteem and self-worth, and how we need to speak kindly to ourselves.

We appreciated that we did indeed have a choice in every aspect of our lives.

In the second section we looked at need to have a clear purpose, to have written goals, and ACTION To-Do lists to help us move forward.

In the third section we looked at the need to keep learning, and have FAITH that we are making progress even when it may appear we are not. To plan our work, and to work our plan. To keep a log or organiser to track our progress. Working smarter not harder, and the incredible power of review. In the fourth section we looked at the value of time and how we view it and use it. How to achieve more by doing less.

In the fifth section we considered how important it is to develop the habit of listening more than we talk, to avoid interrupting otherism and to use open questions.

In the sixth section we saw how money is a secondary result of the primary character development we need to accumulate wealth. We saw that the magic of compound

In the seventh section we discussed the need to take care of your number one priority, your health, for without it, all you finish up with is a row of noughts.

You can become the person you always secretly thought you COULD become.

You can. You really can! It is within your grasp, if you start NOW.

This is Brian Butler, wishing you all the very best for the brightest future of success, wealth, health, and happiness.

APPENDIX

RESOURCE ADDRESSES

TO GET IN CONTACT WITH THE AUTHOR PLEASE VISIT: http://ernestworkman.com

KINESIOLOGY IN GREAT BRITAIN

The Academy of Systematic Kinesiology
Foundation, Professional Certificate and two year Diploma Courses.
https://www.kinesiology.co.uk

KINESIOLOGY IN IRELAND

Association of Systematic Kinesiology (ASK) in Ireland
Kinesiology practitioners and information available
www.Kinesiology.ie
The Academy of Systematic Kinesiology (TASK) in Ireland
Kinesiology training courses throughout Ireland (beginners and diploma)
www.BalancedHealth.ie

≈ NOTES ≈

NOTES

≈ NOTES ≈

≈ NOTES ≈

≈ NOTES ≈

www.ingramcontent.com/pod-product-compliance
Lightning Source LLC
Chambersburg PA
CBHW061110070526
44583CB00027B/3247